Published by

Pedigree®

Books Ltd

under license from

ipc COUNTRY & LEISURE MEDIA

**Pedigree Books Ltd
The Old Rectory
Matford Lane
Exeter
Devon
EX2 4PS**

All Editorial, Design and
Reprographics by Final
Score Ltd.
Tel: ++ 44 (0)1277 632070
Fax: ++ 44 (0)1277 632080
finalscore@compuserve.com
www.fsrsl.co.uk

Photography: Allsport and
Action Images.

™ and © IPC Media Ltd
2001

SHOOT
ANNUAL 2002 INCLUDES...

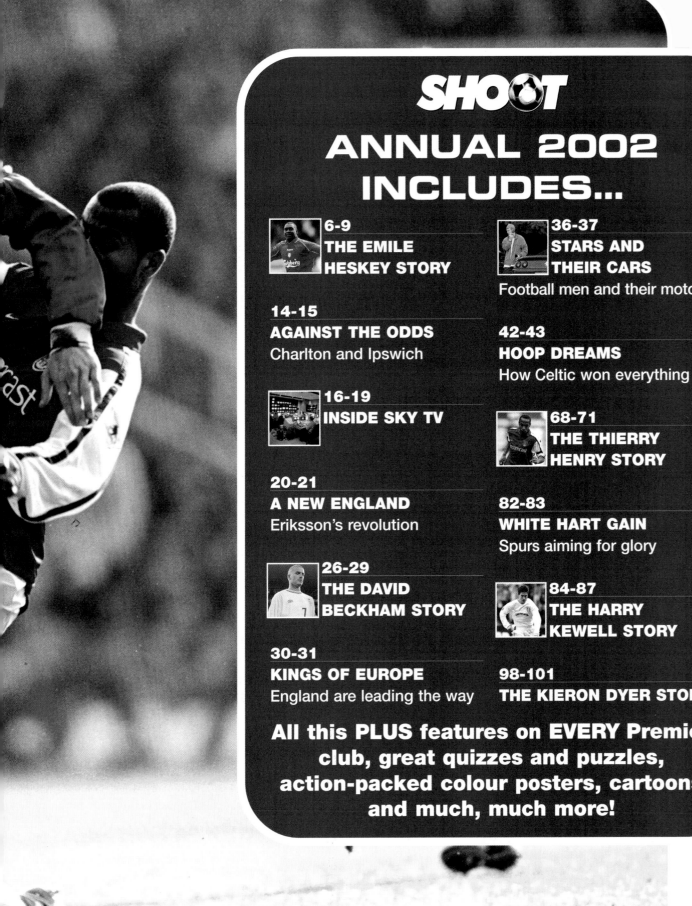
All this PLUS features on EVERY Premier club, great quizzes and puzzles, action-packed colour posters, cartoons and much, much more!

£6.99

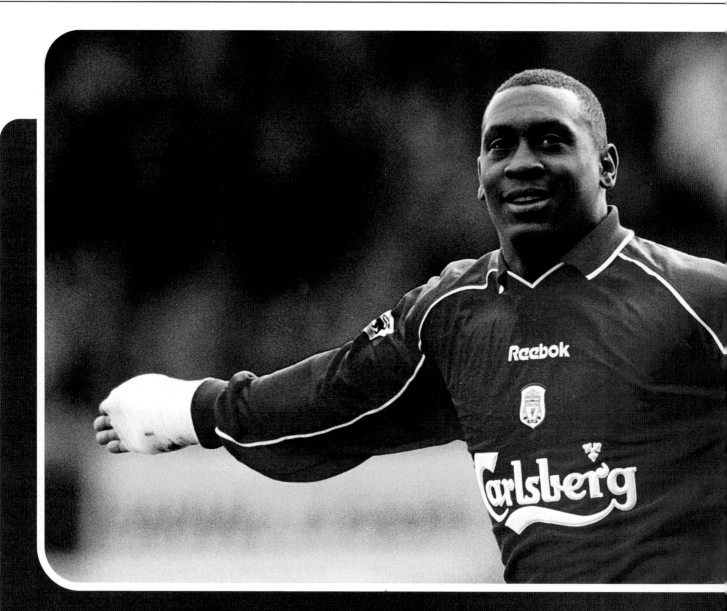

EMILE'S ON WHEELS

What a great season it was for Emile Heskey last time out. Liverpool were the cup aces of the year and Heskey's power play led the way as he threatened to run riot in front of the opposition's goal.

EMILE HESKEY was born in Leicester on January 11th 1978 and was taken to watch his local side, including their goalscoring hero, Gary Lineker. But like many black and Asian kids of his era, Heskey grew up a Liverpool fan and idolised John Barnes. "John Barnes was my hero when I was growing up," says Emile. "I used to love watching him play. I admired Gary Lineker, too. He went to the same school as me and was a bit of a hero for everyone in Leicester."

Even before he left school, Heskey knew that he was going to be a soccer pro. It was his greatest ambition and he played well enough to star for the City of Leicester School and for his Sunday League side, Ratcliffe and Groby. But, believe it or not, the big man was not even considered as a striker in those days. "The school team had two lads who could only play up front, so I had to play in midfield," recalls Heskey. "For my club I played right across the defence, but usually at centre-half."

He had already come to the attention of local club Leicester City, but it was only on turning out for the club's Midlands Youth team as a 15-year-old that he finally settled in up front. "I got a game as a forward, scored a couple of goals and stayed there. Now everyone seems to think I've always been a striker," says the player.

Emile had to do all the usual jobs of a football trainee, like cleaning boots and sweeping the dressing rooms, but not for long as he became a first-team regular while he was still a teenager. He also won England youth caps, but his big moment came on March 8th 1995 when he made his senior debut at Queens Park Rangers. Leicester lost 0-2 but he had a good game. By the end of the following season the supporters realised he was a force to be reckoned with and named him Leicester's Young Player of the Year. "I was always confident I would make it as a professional," he says. "Even when they were letting other kids go. I always worked hard and it paid off in the end."

By then of course he had scored his first senior goal, which came at Norwich on September 30th 1995 when he appeared as sub with three minutes to go and hit the winner.

THE Leicester fans quickly took to their new hero and christened him 'Bruno' - after the former heavyweght boxer - because of his 6ft 2ins, 13st 12lbs frame and his bustling approach to the game. He was never afraid to go in among the flying boots with either his feet or his head.

HESKEY made his Reds debut in a 1-1 draw with Sunderland on March 11th 2000 and scored his first goal for the side on April 1st the same year, in a 3-0 win over Coventry City.

AT Leicester he was mostly used on the left, which is a tribute to his skill because he is naturally right-footed. His first major honour with the Foxes was winning the League Cup in 1997 and Emile even scored one of the goals at Wembley. He was back there in 2000 to win the cup again with Leicester.

QUIZ QUESTION

HIS FULL NAME IS EMILE WILLIAM .... HESKEY. CAN YOU FILL IN THE MISSING MIDDLE NAME? ANSWER AT THE BOTTOM OF THE PAGE.

JUST after that second taste of Wembley glory, Heskey signed for his boyhood heroes, Liverpool, for a huge club record fee of £11m. The Reds had tried to sign the striker a few years earlier but he had turned them down and many people thought Gerard Houllier was crazy to pay such a large amount of money for a young, inexperienced player like Heskey.

SINCE arriving at Anfield he has become a first team regular and has also confirmed his place in the England squad. It was on April 28th 1999 that Heskey made his England debut, having already won 16 caps at U21 level. His first run-out for the senior side came as a sub for Kevin Phillips in a 1-1 draw in Hungary. He started a match for the first time in a friendly against Argentina in February 2000. It was a 0-0 draw, but Emile was named Man of the Match.

EMILE made the England squad for Euro 2000 and played in two of the group matches, both times replacing club-mate Michael Owen. Although he is still only a youngster, Emile Heskey has already won an army of fans as well as a box full of medals and caps. The one medal he wants more than any other, though, is the Premiership title and after his treble trophy haul in 2000/01, who would bet against him picking up the big one in the near future?

HESKEY SIDELINES

HESKEY COMES FROM A FAMILY OF MARKET TRADERS - JUST LIKE HIS HERO, GARY LINEKER, WHOSE DAD STILL OWNS A FRUIT AND VEG STALL AT LEICESTER MARKET.

ALTHOUGH HE IS BIG AND BUSTLING ON THE PITCH, OFF IT HE IS QUIET, WELL-SPOKEN AND ALWAYS VERY POLITE.

HIS FAVOURITE FOOD IS INDIAN, ALTHOUGH HE DOES NOT GET TO EAT IT VERY OFTEN BECAUSE HE HAS TO WATCH HIS DIET AS A PROFESSIONAL SPORTSMAN.

Quiz answer: Ivanhoe

GOLDEN OWEN

England hero Michael Owen struck two goals in the last seven minutes of the game to hand Liverpool the FA Cup at the Millennium Stadium in Cardiff.

It was the Anfield club's second trophy triumph of a glorious season, with the Worthington Cup already tucked safely away in the trophy cabinet and the UEFA Cup soon to follow.

16 mins

the moments that mattered...

16 mins
Thierry Henry's powerful shot deflects wide off the arm of Stephane Henchoz - but ref Steve Dunn awards a goal kick instead of a penalty...or even a corner.

56 mins
The speedy Henry goes close again, but his shot is clawed away by Sander Westerveld and Sami Hyypia clears Ashley Cole's follow-up effort off the line.

68 mins
Another Henry shot is beaten out, this time to Freddie Ljungberg whose lob is headed clear by that man Hyypia.

72 mins
It's 1-0 to the Arsenal, as Ljungberg dances round Westerveld to put the Gunners ahead.

74 mins
Henry has the chance to kill the game off, but Westerveld saves and Hyypia - yet again - clears the follow-up off the line.

83 mins
Michael Owen twists in mid-air to crash in a spectacular, and unlikely, equaliser for Liverpool.

88 mins
It's Owen again. The England man chases Patrik Berger's through ball, beats Lee Dixon and Tony Adams and fires in the winner.

72 mins

88 mins

83 mins

WAYNE BRIDGE
SOUTHAMPTON

WHO WANTS TO BE A
FOOTY-AIRE?

The TV quiz show 'Who Wants To Be A Millionaire' has been one of the most popular things on the box in recent years. Shoot presents a fun football version of the quiz for you to try your luck with.

HOW TO PLAY

Ask a friend to act as question master Chris Tarrant and read out the clues, while you try to answer them.

The more questions you answer, the more successful you and your team will become - right up to helping your country lift the World Cup!

If you get stuck you can ring the coach, ask the crowd or make a substitution, where two of the answers are removed. But remember, you can only use each get-out once in the game - so think carefully!

When you have successfully completed the challenge on this page, turn to p35 for part two!

Ready? Is that your final answer? Then get thinking!

1 Win: Promotion from the Conference
Q. Which Premiership club play their home games at Old Trafford?

- A. Manchester City
- B. Manchester Rovers
- C. Manchester Ship Canal
- D. Manchester United

2 Win: Promotion from Division Three
Q. Who is the manager of England?

- A. Erik Goram Svensson
- B. Steen Govan Ekstrom
- C. Sven Goran Eriksson
- D. Sven Erik Goransson

3 Win: The LDV Vans Trophy
Q. What is the nickname of West Ham?

- A. Hammers
- B. Spanners
- C. Chisels
- D. Nails

4 Win: Promotion from Division Two
Q. What is the christian name of Desailly at Chelsea?

- A. Manuel
- B. Marcel
- C. Marco
- D. Molly

Answers on page 110-111

QUESTION 1

A B C D
ASK THE CROWD
SUB: Answers c and d are left.
PHONE THE COACH: d

QUESTION 2

A B C D
ASK THE CROWD
SUB: Answers a and c are left.
PHONE THE COACH: c

QUESTION 3

A B C D
ASK THE CROWD
SUB: Answers a and b are left.
PHONE THE COACH: a

QUESTION 4

A B C D
ASK THE CROWD
SUB: Answers b and d are left.
PHONE THE COACH: b

AGAINST THE ODDS

The 'experts' said they would go straight back down. But Ipswich and Charlton defied the critics to storm up the Premiership last season. Shoot pays tribute to the little guys who upset the odds...

Recent seasons have seen many newly-promoted clubs struggle to make an impact in the top flight, with plenty losing their new found status after just one season up among the big boys.

There was little reason to think that Ipswich Town and Charlton Athletic would be any different in 2000/01 - but by the end of thrilling campaigns for both clubs, Town were celebrating qualifying for Europe, while the Addicks had enjoyed their most successful season for many years.

So what was the secret? Teamwork was the key for both clubs, with the existing squads strengthened after promotion, but not dramatically so.

Claus Jensen, from Bolton, and Glasgow Rangers striker Jonatan Johanssen moved to The Valley, while giant defender Hermann Hreidarsson was Ipswich's big buy, signing from Wimbledon for £4m.

But no big name superstars on huge wages were brought in, and the new arrivals were allowed to slot in to an already well-established team pattern. Playing neat and tidy football and working hard for each other allowed both clubs to surprise opponents and fans alike with their bright attacking skills and a refusal to be easily beaten.

"I said at the start of the season that it would be a great achievement if all three of the newly-promoted sides could stay in the Premiership, as it has never been done before," recalls highly-rated Charlton manager Alan Curbishley (pictured above).

"Unfortunately Manchester City didn't manage it, but obviously I was delighted we retained our place.

"Great credit must also go to Ipswich. They did fantastically well and surprised everybody, probably including themselves.

"Stability is the key ingredient and in the last five or six years, both Charlton and Ipswich have

demonstrated how clubs like ours should be run."

And Ipswich Town boss George Burley (pic left) - voted Manager of the Year for his efforts - agrees, saying: "Both of our clubs did well and exceeded the expectations of other people last season.

"Like us, I'm sure Charlton would have happily settled for 17th place before the season started, but they are a good side who work hard for each other and it brought them a lot of success.

"For us, to qualify for Europe was nothing short of phenomenal.

"We showed great consistency and were in the top six for most of the campaign, so it was not down to good luck or one run of form."

How Blackburn, Bolton and Fulham will be hoping to emulate the feats of Charlton and Ipswich in this season's FA Premiership.

GOING UP? GOING DOWN!

Here's how the promoted clubs have fared in the Premiership in recent seasons...

ADDICK ACE
CLAUS JENSEN

A skilful midfielder with an eye for goal, this Denmark international turned down a host of interested clubs - including fellow Premiership new boys Ipswich - to join Charlton from Bolton Wanderers for £4m in the summer of 2000. It turned out to be an excellent move for both club and player, as Jensen emerged as a gifted playmaker with excellent passing and dribbling skills, as well as a danger from dead-ball situations, as Charlton surged up the Premiership.

TOWN STAR
HERMANN HREIDARSSON

This giant Iceland international had already been relegated twice from the top flight, with Palace and Wimbledon, before joining Ipswich in a £4m deal on the eve of the 2000/01 season. Happy playing in the centre of defence or wide on the left, his strength and composure at the back, and his willingness to push forward in support of his attack, made him one of the Premiership's star turns last year.

2000/2001

Promoted	Final Position
Charlton	9th
Man City	18th (relegated)
Ipswich	5th

1999/2000

Promoted	Final Position
Sunderland	7th
Bradford	17th
Watford	20th (relegated)

1998/1999

Promoted	Final Position
Nott'm For	20th (relegated)
Middlesbro'	9th
Charlton	18th (relegated)

1997/1998

Promoted	Final Position
Bolton	18th (relegated)
Barnsley	19th (relegated)
C. Palace	20th (relegated)

1996/1997

Promoted	Final Position
Sunderland	18th (relegated)
Derby	12th
Leicester	9th

REACH FOR THE
SKY

SKY SPORTS

There has been a revolution in the world of televised football since Sky took over exclusive broadcasting rights to the Premiership in 1992. All the channels have fine-tuned their operations over the last decade, but it is still Sky who lead the way.

It is largely thanks to Sky television that English football can now compete financially with the best in the world.

Thanks to the hundreds of millions of pounds invested into the sport by the TV station, and the high profile their dedicated coverage has helped produce, the domestic game can now count itself among the biggest on the planet.

Football has always been hugely popular in this country - as proved by the long-running success of magazines such as Shoot - but since the Sky TV revolution it has moved onto another level.

Top British clubs can now stand toe-to-toe with their Italian and Spanish rivals, offering huge incentives for the top players to come to these shores.

It is amazing to think that when Sky launched there were fears that it could ruin the game, with supporters staying away in droves. Instead, average top flight attendances have risen from 21,622 in 1991 to more than 30,000 last term.

The BBC, ITV, Channel Five, onDigital and the rest have all improved their coverage as a result, but it is Sky who set the standard.

Everything looks sleek and sharp when the football comes onto our screens, but behind the scenes there have been many days of careful planning and hard work by a 100-strong crew of staff, including technicians, cameramen, presenters, statisticians, drivers, producers, editors and the match director.

At seven o'clock on a typical Monday matchday, everyone holds their breath as the previous few days' hard work comes to a head and the match presentation begins, with presenters Richard Keys and Andy Gray welcoming the viewing public to the game - via the Astra satellite, whirring away some 23,500 miles above the earth!

Here's a look at what goes into getting a match from the ground and onto your television set...

ON THE ROAD

A typical Premiership match will have up to 100 crew members working on it, with the game broadcast direct from the ground, rather than a studio.

At the heart of the Outside Broadcast (OB) is the fleet of up to 10 trucks and support vehicles - including a catering wagon - based at the ground. The four most crucial are...

VAN ONE
THE PRESENTATION SCANNER
This is where the match build-up, half-time and full-time coverage is produced by the programme director and his team.

VAN TWO
MATCH SCANNER
This is where the match director selects the camera angles and controls the cameramen and commentators during the game.

VAN THREE
VTR SCANNER
Full of technicians and video machines covering every camera in the ground. There are usually 18 camera positions, although some big games have seen Sky use 32! All incidents are recorded and ready for instant playback from loads of angles.

VAN FOUR
LINKS TRUCK
This is the truck that sends the pictures and sound out of the ground and into your home. The pictures travel around 50,000 miles before popping up on screen, though! They travel from the truck to Telecom Tower in London, into Sky and are then beamed up to the Astra satellite before arriving in your living room a fraction of a second later!

FIVE SKY FOOTIE FACTS

1 The first hat-trick on Sky was scored by Mark Robins, for Norwich against Oldham in November 1992.

2 The most common scoreline is 1-1.

3 In almost ten years of broadcasting, two matches have been lost to floodlight failure - West Ham v C. Palace and Wimbledon v Arsenal, both in 1997. It turned out that a betting syndicate had arranged for the lights to be switched out at both matches!

4 Sky screened their 500th 'live' game in November 2000 - Chelsea v Leeds

5 The first sending-off in a televised match was Nigel Winterburn, of Arsenal, against Liverpool in January 1993.

Of course, it's not just the great pictures that make watching a 'live' match on TV a thrilling event - the sound is dead important too.

For a big game there can be up to 20 directional microphones placed around the stadium to pick up all the noise and drama on the pitch and in the stands...with the rude bits edited out, of course!

All live matches are produced on a system called Dolby Surround Sound™, so subscribers with the right equipment can actually feel as if they are in the stadium itself, with noise coming from all around.

Add to that the atmospheric music often used during the build-up and closing titles and it makes for an exciting evening's entertainment watching a big game.

It's almost as good as actually being there!

HE'S ANDY WITH THE GADGETS

Co-presenter Andy Gray won some of the game's highest honours as a player with the likes of Aston Villa, Everton, Wolves and Scotland - but he is now as famous off the pitch as the man who controls all of Sky's funky new electronic gadgets.

No longer do we just cheer a goal, we get to see how hard the ball was struck, how far out the scorer was and the name on his underpants!

But, amazingly, Gray has never had the opportunity to get used to the new kit before going live with it.

He says: "I got into the technology simply because we wanted to change the way to view the game at home and give people more options.

"It wasn't a case of choosing it. It was more a matter of them coming to me and saying, `Right Andy, here is a new piece of technology, get on with it'."

"I had to learn it as I was doing it. There was no ten-week course.

"It happened again quite recently with the touch screen we use for Monday Night Football.

"I walked into the office one Monday and saw the piece of kit at 3pm and by 7pm I was working it live on television. That's what is expected of us!"

The new style of football coverage Sky pioneered is now copied through television and every time Gray sees a Sky idea ripped off, he smiles.

"We have done so much and pushed the barriers back so far.

"Now we're no longer regarded as a cowboy outfit in television as we were when we started.

"We've gone from being the outsider to being the forerunner that everyone judges themselves against."

SVEN'S NEW ENGLAND

England broke with more than 100 years of tradition in November 2000 by appointing a foreign manager to the national side. The Shoot Annual sees how Sven Goran Eriksson is getting on with the job...

The appointment of Sweden's Sven Goran Eriksson to succeed Kevin Keegan as England boss caused surprise right across Europe.

Many people felt that the job should only go to an Englishman, such as former boss Terry Venables, while others argued that the FA were right to bring in the best man for the job - regardless of which country he happened to be born in.

"I think I am like most people in thinking that having an English manager would be nice," explained midfielder Frank Lampard at the time. "But maybe that's more for tradition than anything else. Success on the field has to be the most important thing."

So it was that the man who had guided Italian club Lazio to the domestic 'double' the previous season became the 10th full-time coach of the national side.

An intelligent man with a fantastic football pedigree but little in-depth knowledge of the English game, Eriksson promptly set about taking in as many Premiership matches as possible and, together with his assistant Tord Grip, began to compile a dossier of our top stars.

In several cases the results of their research was surprising. The first squad announced by the Swede, for a friendly against Spain, included some unfamiliar names.

Alongside the likes of Beckham and Owen were left-sided wing-backs Chris Powell, 31, of Charlton, and Everton's Michael Ball, as well as midfielder Gavin McCann of Sunderland.

But there could be no arguing with Eriksson's choices as all three enjoyed excellent international debuts.

"People told me there were no left-backs in England, but I've found five," explained Eriksson when asked about Powell and Ball. "Everyone has been extremely positive and helpful.

"Chances like this - to manage a great country like England - do not come up very often in life, so I am delighted to have the opportunity.

"The most important thing is to create a good group of people who are going to love the English team. If you don't have that, you will never get good results.

"But the standard is high and the future is very good for England."

England Managers
and how they started

ERA	MANAGER	RECORD	FIRST GAME
1946-62	Walter Winterbottom	(P139, W78, D33, L28)	v N.Ireland, W7-2
1963-74	Sir Alf Ramsey	(P113, W69, D27, L17)	v France, W5-2
1974	c/t - Joe Mercer	(P7, W3, D3, L1)	v Wales, W2-0
1974-77	Don Revie	(P29, W14, D8, L7)	v Czechoslovakia, W3-0
1977-82	Ron Greenwood	(P55, W33, D12, L10)	v Switzerland, D0-0
1982-90	Bobby Robson	(P95, W47, D30, L18)	v Denmark, D2-2
1990-93	Graham Taylor	(P38, W18, D13, L7)	v Hungary, W1-0
1994-96	Terry Venables	(P23, W11, D11, L1)	v Denmark, W1-0
1996-99	Glenn Hoddle	(P23, W14, D5, L4)	v Moldova, W3-0
1999	c/t - Howard Wilkinson	(P1, W0, D0, L1)	v France, L0-2
1999-2000	Kevin Keegan	(P15, W6, D7, L2)	v Poland, W3-1
2000	c/t - Howard Wilkinson	(P1, W0, D1, L0)	v Finland, D0-0
2000	c/t - Peter Taylor	(P1, W0, D0, L1)	v Italy, L0-1
Nov 2000	Sven Goran Eriksson		v Spain, W3-0

(c/t = caretaker manager)

SHOOT inter@ctive

THE NAME GAME

Read the clues and see if you can suss out the identity of the mystery players...

1

_ _ C _ _ E _   _ _ E _

- I play for a team in red
* I've won caps for my country
- My international debut was against Chile in 1998
* I scored a wonder goal against Argentina in the 1998 World Cup
- I've advertised crisps on television

2

_ _ _ D _   _ A _
_ I _ _ _ R _ _ _

* I used to play for PSV Eindhoven
- I am a Dutch international
* I cost my English club a then record £19m when I signed.
- Jaap Stam is an international and club team-mate of mine

QUICK FIRE ROUND

GIVE YOURSELF A MINUTE - OR 60 SECONDS IF YOU'RE FEELING UP TO IT - AND SEE HOW MANY OF THE FOLLOWING TOP FLIGHT QUESTIONS YOU CAN GET RIGHT...

1 Which club is managed by Sam Allardyce?

2 From which club did Danny Murphy join Liverpool?

3 Name the side that play their home matches at Pride Park

4 Is Ashley Cole (pic right) a left-back or a right-back?

5 Which club are nicknamed The Foxes?

6 Sasa Ilic plays in goal for which Premiership team?

7 Their last three managers were: Graeme Souness, Dave Jones and Glenn Hoddle. Which club is it?

8 Who would you be watching in action if you saw Svensson score past Gerrard?

9 Which club does Sean Davis play for?

10 Who was voted as England's Young Player of the Year last season?

COLOUR 'EM IN

ooops! There was a mistake at the printers and all the colour got drained out of this picture of Aston Villa's Alpay and Jimmy Floyd Hasselbaink of Chelsea. Show us your colouring skills by brightening up the picture with your own great look for the players!

Quiz Answers on pp110/111

WORTHINGTON CUP WINNERS
LIVERPOOL

2000/01's GLORY BOYS

CIS Insurance Cup winners CELTIC

Scottish Cup winners CELTIC

LDV Vans Trophy Winners PORT VALE

SIMPLY THE BECKS!

Yes, it's Becks! Couldn't leave out England's best known player and the national captain, could we? Little did he know when he first kicked a ball around in his garden where it would all end up.

DAVID BECKHAM was born on May 2nd, 1975 in Leytonstone, East London, not far from the Leyton Orient and West Ham grounds. But the number one club in the Beckham household was Manchester United and David soon became a big fan of the Old Trafford club. He even wore a United shirt to training when he was asked to attend sessions at Tottenham Hotspur!

David's first teams were his school sides, Chase Lane Junior and Chingford High, and also the local park outfit Ridgeway Rovers. When he won a Bobby Charlton soccer skills award in 1986 and was mascot for United when they played at West Ham in 1987 there was no question where he was going to start his soccer career. "All I ever wanted to do was play for Manchester United - and the dream came true," says Beckham today. "There was never another team for me."

Having been spotted by United's London scout, Malcolm Fidgeon, Becks signed trainee forms with the club in July 1991 and after winning the FA Youth Cup in May 1992 he made his first-team debut in October 1992 against Brighton, as sub for Andrei Kanchelskis. But it was not until January 23rd, 1993 that he signed as a full professional.

A young Beckham in action for United

With wife Victoria and son Brooklyn

THE debuts came thick and fast for David as his career unfolded. He trained a lot with Man United legend Eric Cantona, who helped him improve his skills. In December 1994, at the age of 19, he made his Champions' League debut and scored in a 4-0 win over Turkish giants Galatasaray.

ONE of the highlights of his career is this sensational goal he scored against Wimbledon on the opening day of 1996/97. He took a shot from inside his own half and it flew past the Dons' 'keeper Neil Sullivan to clinch a 3-0 win. David Beckham had truly arrived.

THAT was even before he made his League debut, which he did while on loan to Preston. That game was on March 4th 1995 and Becks went on to score twice in five games for the Deepdale club. "It was great and opened my eyes to how lucky I was to be playing at a club like Manchester United," he says.

BECKHAM'S senior Premiership debut came on April 2nd 1995 in a 0-0 draw at home to Leeds United. Anyone trying to give a commentary on his fast-moving career would run out of breath as the midfielder began his international days in England's youth and then under-21 sides. It seemed certain to be only a matter of time before he made his senior debut for the national team.

A few weeks later, on September 1st, 1996, David made his full England debut in a 3-0 World Cup qualifying win away to Moldova. He has been going strong since, with appearances in the 1998 World Cup and Euro 2000. The spotlight was turned on him when he was sent-off in the 1998 World Cup but he overcame that and has since been made captain of his country - another dream realised.

HE is famed for his amazing free-kick skills but he is also the most dangerous ball-crosser in Britain if not in Europe. Although there has been much talk about him playing in Italy or Spain he has always said that he is happy in the north west of England with wife Victoria and son Brooklyn and does not want to play for anyone other than Manchester United.

BECKHAM SIDELINES

BECKS LIKES HOLIDAYS IN THE CARIBBEAN BUT HE ALSO ENJOYS MALTA AND IRELAND AND HAS EVEN BEEN TO CLACTON A FEW TIMES!

HE CANNOT STAND BAD MANNERS AND IS ALWAYS VERY POLITE. HE IS ALWAYS ONE OF THE LAST PLAYERS TO LEAVE THE TRAINING GROUND BECAUSE HE TRIES TO SIGN AS MANY AUTOGRAPHS AS POSSIBLE.

HIS FAMILY STILL GO TO SEE NEARLY ALL OF HIS GAMES.

WITH Manchester United he has won countless medals, including five Premiership titles, two FA Cups, the European Champions' League and two Charity Shields. In addition, he was named Young Player of the Year in 1997 - not a bad list of honours for a player still only in his mid-20s!

Quiz answer: Joseph

LIVERPOOL'S UEFA CUP TRIUMPH MAKES ENGLAND...
KINGS OF

ENGLISH football proved it is once again a force to be reckoned with as four Premier League clubs blazed a trail in the European competitions last season.

Back in the late-1970s and early-1980s English teams were the toast of Europe. No other country came close to matching our achievements and between 1977 and 1984 an English name appeared on the European Cup in an astonishing seven out of eight seasons, with Liverpool, Nottingham Forest and Aston Villa all lifting the trophy.

And now the English are back in the Euro big time. Man United, Arsenal and Leeds all flew the flag in last season's Champions' League, with the Elland Road outfit going all the way to the Semi-Finals in a campaign that saw them beat off challenges from the likes of AC Milan and Lazio.

But it was Gerard Houllier's Liverpool cup kings who proved the most successful of them all by bringing home the silverware.

After a break of 17 years, the Mersey Reds confirmed their return as one of Europe's top clubs by clinching the 2000/01 UEFA Cup in dramatic fashion.

With the FA and Worthington Cups already safely locked away in the Anfield trophy room, Liverpool - inspired by midfield playmaker Gary McAllister - eventually won a thrilling match against Spanish side Alaves 5-4 in extra-time for their first continental success since clinching the European Cup against Roma back in 1984.

That victory - their third in the UEFA Cup - underlines Liverpool's record as England's top European performers. As well as those three UEFA Cups (1973, 1976 and 2001) the club has also lifted the European Cup on four occasions (1977, 1978, 1981, 1984) and the European Super Cup once (1977).

And Michael Owen and Co. certainly earned their trophy the hard way, knocking out the likes of Greek side Olympiakos, Serie A table-toppers Roma and Spanish giants Barcelona on the way.

"It is an historic day, I am so proud," said Liverpool boss Gerard Houllier after the game.

"This team will go on to become immortal. We are always being compared to the great Liverpool sides of the past - but now we have written our own page in the club's history."

TOP OF THE PILE

Following on from Man United's triumph in the 1999 Champions' League, Liverpool's victory takes England back to the top of the table of European winners. Here's how the top five looks...

Country	European Cup	Cup-Winners' Cup	UEFA Cup	Total
England	9	8	10	27
Italy	9	7	10	26
Spain	9	7	8	24
Germany	6	4	6	16
Holland	6	1	3	10

Scotland lie eighth equal with the former Soviet Union in the table, both countries having won three European trophies.

EUROPE

Leeds United's Alan Smith scores past Lazio 'keeper Angelo Peruzzi in last season's Champions' League

FOOTBALL CRAZY!

Wonderful, weird, wacky and more besides. Football can thrill and excite us with its brilliance or leave us laughing our heads off at its stupidity. Here's a look at some crazy - but true - stories...

DYER CONSEQUENCES

Newcastle and England star Kieron Dyer has certainly been putting the wind up opposing defenders with some of his brilliant displays over the last couple of seasons.

And the wicked 20 year-old told Shoot the secret behind keeping other teams' players at a good distance.

"I've been given this new energy drink to try at Newcastle," he explained. "But all it does is give me the farts all the time!"

THE LAST POST

In the 1997/98 season, First Division Ipswich Town called in a local witch doctor to have a quiet word with one of their goalposts!

The post in question, at what is now the South Stand end of the ground, had been responsible for keeping out several vital 'goals'.

The first biggie was in the previous season's Play-Off Semi-Final and another was in a tightly-fought Coca-Cola Cup-tie with Chelsea.

The witch doctor performed a ritual dance to bring good luck back to the post, threatening to turn it into firewood if anything else went wrong!

CHINESE TAKEAWAY

There are a lot of arguments about how football came to be invented, and one theory holds ancient Chinese soldiers responsible.

Legend has it that when the Chinese armies were off on away trips conquering foreign lands they used to cut off the heads of their beaten opponents and kick them around the battlegrounds for a laugh.

It gives a whole new meaning to losing your head in front of goal!

SUB STANDARD

Substitutes can often make a dramatic contribution to a game - coming on and changing the course of events with a well timed shot or pass.

But few subs have made quite such an impact as Notts County midfielder Andy Hughes managed last season.

Hughes came on as a last minute sub for County as they were trailing Wigan 2-1 in a crucial Division Two match.

In the space of sixty seconds he scored from a rebound off his own penalty-kick and then got sent-off for fighting!

DIVINE INTERVENTION

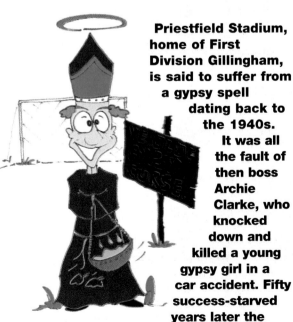

Priestfield Stadium, home of First Division Gillingham, is said to suffer from a gypsy spell dating back to the 1940s.

It was all the fault of then boss Archie Clarke, who knocked down and killed a young gypsy girl in a car accident. Fifty success-starved years later the Gills appointed a Catholic priest called Kevin McElhinney to drive out the curse... and promptly won their next three home games, eventually ending up in the First Division for the first time in their history!

PLOUGHING FORWARD

Wolves goalkeeper Mike Stowell was dead excited when he got called up to the England 'B' squad for a match against Algeria in December 1990.

But when he woke up in the morning to travel to the airport and catch his flight to North Africa there was one slight problem - it was tipping down with snow and it was impossible to drive on the roads.

It didn't stop Mike, though. He borrowed a snow plough and drove to the airport in that!

Artwork: Barry Holmes, barry@meta-gb.com

TEDDY SHERINGHAM

proudly shows off his PFA Players' Player of the Year award. The England striker also picked up the Football Writers' Footballer of the Year trophy, becoming the second successive Man United player to do the 'double' after Roy Keane in 2000. Now Sheri's at Spurs and looking for more glory.

WHO WANTS TO BE A FOOTY-AIRE?

It's the second part of the brilliant Shoot quiz. You can phone the coach, ask the crowd or use a sub if you get stuck, but you can only use each escape route once before your game is over. Turn to page 75 for part three.

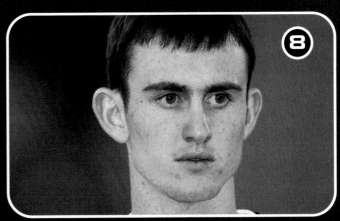

⑧

5 ▸ **Win: Promotion from Division One**
Q. Who won the Champions' League last season?

- A. Real Madrid
- B. Valencia
- C. Bayern Munich
- D. Liverpool

6 ▸ **Win: The Worthington Cup**
Q. What number shirt does David Beckham wear?

- A. 6
- B. 7
- C. 8
- D. 10

7 ▸ **Win: The FA Cup**
Q. Who finished top scorer in the Premiership in 2000/2001?

- A. Marcus Stewart
- B. Jimmy Floyd Hasselbaink
- C. Thierry Henry
- D. Henrik Larsson

8 ▸ **Win: Footballer of the Year award**
Q. From which club did Francis Jeffers join Arsenal?

- A. Everton
- B. Liverpool
- C. Tottenham
- D. Middlesbrough

Answers on page 110-111

QUESTION 5
PHONE THE COACH: c
SUB: Answers a and c are left.
ASK THE CROWD
A B C D

QUESTION 6
PHONE THE COACH: b
SUB: Answers b and c are left.
ASK THE CROWD
A B C D

QUESTION 7
PHONE THE COACH: b
SUB: Answers b and d are left.
ASK THE CROWD
A B C D

QUESTION 8
PHONE THE COACH: a
SUB: Answers a and d are left.
ASK THE CROWD
A B C D

STARS AND THEIR CARS

Good acceleration, a great engine and useful on corners - and that's just David Beckham. For today's football stars, a flash motor comes second only to a boot sponsorship deal and a trophy girlfriend. Here's a look at what some of the top fellas are chucking their dirty socks into the boot of to drive down to the launderette...

PAUL SCHOLES

SCHOLESY shows off the accessory that every young man about town must have these days - no, not the mobile, the £150,000 supercar. In the England man's case it's a gleaming red and black Ferrari - to match the colours of his club side Manchester United. That'll keep Sir Alex of Fergie happy.

JEFF WHITLEY

SLEEK lines, excellent engineering - why it's Man City midfielder Jeff Whitley and his trusty BMW. Jeff was one of the few stars of City's dismal Premiership campaign last season and the Northern Ireland international is sure to be a driving force once again this time around as City battle for a return to the top flight.

DAVID BECKHAM

Flash geezer, flash wheels. Becks loves his cars and is always buying new ones. "I like changing cars and if I can afford it I'll keep doing it. It isn't a crime to have a nice car," he says. The current "nice car" for Becks is a shiny silver Ferrari, as well as a 4WD off-roader and a brand new BMW for the wife.

RORY DELAP

WITH his pace down the flanks it's no surprise to see Derby and Rep of Ireland man Rory Delap in a sporty Subaru Prezza P1. "It's the car I've always wanted," explains Rory. "I've got a real interest in rally cars. My dad and uncle are into the sport. I've had a go and it's harder than it looks."

ANDY COLE

HAVE kit, will travel. Goal king Cole prepares to saddle up and ride out of town in his plush convertible Mercedes Benz. Smooth, classy, quick and efficient - that's man and machine in perfect harmony. All of the Man United stars seem to like their upmarket motors, with the car park at Old Trafford looking like the forecourt of a posh garage at times.

FRANK SINCLAIR

Leicester's Frank Sinclair decked out his swanky Jaguar with a load of gear to make his trips that little bit more enjoyable. The car boasts a DVD, PlayStation, video player and screens in the back of the seats, as well as a banging stereo system. It's all topped off with a chauffer, so Frank can enjoy his little luxuries.

THE BOYS DONE GOOD

They are the young stars who are rocking football. Ten players who have come up through the ranks to force their way into the Premiership and beyond.

1 JOE COLE
WEST HAM

WEST Ham have always encouraged their youngsters to play the game the 'right way' and rewarded exciting talent with a chance in the first-team.

The Hammers squad of recent seasons has been no exception, with the likes of Frank Lampard and Rio Ferdinand making big names for themselves and rocketing from Upton Park to the England squad.

But the brightest lights of the last couple of years - more exciting even than the £18m Ferdinand - have been teenage midfielders Joe Cole and Michael Carrick.

The pair lined-up together in the full England side for last May's friendly with Mexico and look set for a long international future together.

While the Newcastle-born Carrick has been a revelation with his tough-tackling and good distribution, it is the brilliant Cole who has really captured the imagination.

With a bag of tricks to make a top magician jealous, Cole can open up even the tightest of defences with his great vision, superb touch and ability to try the unexpected.

He made his debut as a substitute for Eyal Berkovic in an FA Cup Third Round tie against Swansea City in January 1999 and even a broken leg, suffered in a match against Derby in April 2000, has not prevented him from making his mark and pushing himself into Sven Goran Eriksson's England plans.

"It's amazing to be involved with England - a dream really, and it's something I really want to make the most of," says the player.

2 STEVEN GERRARD
LIVERPOOL

VOTED last season's Young Player of the Year, Steven Gerrard is a tough-tackling, hard-running central midfielder who has replaced the likes of Paul Ince and David Batty in the England set-up.

As well as his strength and power, the Liverpool man, who can also operate in defence, is a good passer of the ball and boasts a thumping shot for good measure.

With three trophies stashed in his cabinet after Liverpool's amazing season in 2000/01, and his England career already well underway, young Steven seems set for a golden future.

"I think he is an all-round player, the type who can do everything well," explains England coach Sven Goran Eriksson.

"He has everything a midfielder needs. You can put him almost anywhere and he will do a good job."

As for the player himself, Steven insists he still has plenty of work to do before he can rest on his laurels.

"I'm not a finished player," he says. "But as long as I prepare myself properly and keep wanting to learn then I can only get better."

A scary thought for his opponents.

3 ASHLEY COLE
ARSENAL

COLE seems to be the name to have if you want to make it into the England squad these days.

There's West Ham's Joe, of course, and then there is striker Andy from Man United. Now comes the third king Cole, Arsenal's exciting left-sided wing-back Ashley, who burst into Sven Goran Eriksson's side late last season.

Having been groomed at Arsenal, Cole first began to get attention across London at Crystal Palace, where he enjoyed a successful spell on loan in 1999/2000.

Quick to get forward, with good ball skills and a strong tackle, Cole has long been groomed to step into Arsenal's legendary back line, and the youngster also seems to have solved the long-running problem at left-back for his country.

"I'm still amazed by it all," admits Cole. "Just to be travelling on the same coach as the Arsenal players is like a dream come true. You learn so much just training with players like Tony Adams and Silvinho.

"And playing for England is everything I dreamed about and more. But now I've got the taste I want more."

4 ALAN SMITH
LEEDS UTD

A quick and aggressive striker who emerged as a star for Leeds as they stormed to the Champions' League Semi-Finals last season.

Snapped up by the Elland Road club as a schoolboy, Alan is not afraid to put his head in where it hurts and has an eye for goal and two good feet that make him a threat from anywhere.

A regular at Under-21 level, he was called into the senior side for the first time for May 2001's friendly with Mexico at Pride Park and made a promising debut as a half-time sub for Michael Owen in the 4-0 victory.

Dogged by disciplinary problems throughout his career, if he can keep his temper in check, Alan is sure to become an important member of the national squad for years to come.

5 OWEN HARGREAVES
BAYERN MUNICH

MANY supporters believed that an Englishman would get his hands on the Champions' League trophy in 2000/01, and they were proved right.

But the man in question did not play for Man United, Leeds or even Arsenal, but for German giants Bayern Munich, who pipped Valencia to lift the continent's most important club trophy.

Little known midfielder Owen Hargreaves - born in Canada to an English dad and Welsh mum - provided a star turn in the Final to underline his man of the match performance against Real Madrid in the semis.

Already an England U21 player, there were even calls to include him in the full England squad so impressive was his play.

With rumours beginning to circulate that several of the big Premiership outfits were interested in signing the youngster, Bayern acted quickly to extend Owen's contract in a bid to keep him in Germany for the next four years.

"At the moment I'm happy here things are going well and I feel at home," admits Hargreaves. "This is my fourth season in Munich, I've kind of grown up here.

"But everyone has their dreams and I'd like to play in the Premiership one day, because it's a great League and my dad would be so proud of me - he wants me to sign for Bolton, where he had trials himself a few years ago!"

6 JOHN TERRY
CHELSEA

ONE of the few English players to shine at Stamford Bridge in recent years, John is a central defender with pace, poise and strength.

Having made his Chelsea debut as a substitute for Dan Petrescu in a Worthington Cup-tie with Aston Villa in October 1998, John progressed to the point of winning his debut England U21 cap early last season, as well as scoring his first League goal for the Blues, in a 1-1 draw at Arsenal in January 2001.

The arrival of Italian boss Claudio Ranieri last season saw John begin to establish himself at the Bridge, where he made 22 Premiership appearances in 2000/01, and he could be the rock on which Chelsea build their side for many years to come.

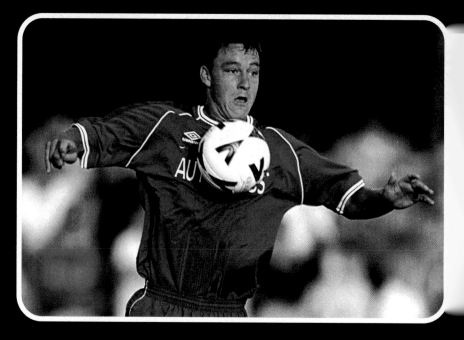

7 TITUS BRAMBLE
IPSWICH TOWN

THERE are few clubs in Europe that can match Ipswich for producing quality young players.

Over the past 30 years or so, the Portman Road outfit have been churning out stars with startling regularity, including England aces Kieron Dyer and Richard Wright.

The latest to roll off the production line is teenager Titus Bramble, a man-mountain who announced his arrival in the Premiership last season with a thumping tackle on Roy Keane.

Bramble continued to show his power throughout the campaign, as well as a calmness on the ball and willingness to pass his way out of trouble that had the critics purring.

His class displays as Town surged into the UEFA Cup earned him an England U21 call-up as well as many top level admirers.

"He's massive, very powerful," says Arsenal striker Thierry Henry. "He's just starting out, but I can tell you he is a very good player.

"I used to play all the time against Marcel Desailly and Bramble is very similar."

8 LUKE CHADWICK
MAN UNITED

THERE can't be too many players who celebrate their first season as a first-team regular by lifting the Premiership title - but that's exactly what young Manchester United winger Luke Chadwick managed last season.

Capped at England U21 level even before he forced his way into the Old Trafford senior side, the highly-rated Luke is happy playing on either flank and provides some stiff competition for the likes of Ryan Giggs, David Beckham and Paul Scholes.

After a successful spell gaining experience on loan at Belgian side Royal Antwerp, Luke returned to Manchester last season and set about forcing his way into Sir Alex Ferguson's plans.

"It still hasn't really sunk in yet," admits the player. "To come back from Antwerp and win my first League Championship was an incredible achievement.

"I've just got to go on now and try to get as many appearances under my belt as possible this season."

9 GARETH BARRY
ASTON VILLA

HE seems to have been around for years already, but England defender Gareth Barry is still only just into his 20s.

Snapped up from Nationwide League side Brighton while still a schoolboy, Gareth has long been tipped for the top and benefitted from playing alongside England pair Gareth Southgate and Ugo Ehiogu at Villa Park.

Happy playing in central defence, at sweeper or on the left side, he is cool and calm on the ball and reads the game brilliantly.

He made his England senior debut against the Ukraine in May 2000 and, although he returned to the U21s to continue learning his trade, he seems certain to play a major part in Sven Goran Eriksson's national revolution.

"To be honest, he is phenomenal," says Barry's club boss, John Gregory. "I sometimes think that I don't want to heap too much praise onto him, but he is unfazed by it all. He just gets on with things."

10 ADAM MURRAY
DERBY COUNTY

THERE is a revolution going on at Pride Park, where Derby's latest crop of talented young stars are pushing hard to establish themselves in the first-team.

Striker Malcolm Christie has already broken through, while midfielder Adam Murray is also making quite a name for himself.

Murray's style can best be summed up by the fact that he names Paul Gascoigne and Paul Ince as his heroes - he's a strong ball-winner with excellent skills, who can sit back and protect the defence or get forward well.

Already a member of the England U21 set-up, Murray is convinced that training with the cream of the country's young players can only be a benefit. "It makes you twice the player," he says. "The quality out there is unbelievable."

And at club level, too, Murray sees better times ahead after last season's relegation scrap.

"There are a lot of good young lads coming through at Derby," he reveals. "With the quality we've got, this season should turn out to be a good one."

MARTIN O'NEILL

holds up the Scottish Championship trophy after leading Celtic to treble glory in his first season at Parkhead.

HOOP DREAMS

Celtic stormed back to the top of the Scottish charts last season by winning all three domestic trophies north of the border. After several years away the Bhoys are back in town.

WHAT a difference a year makes! In May 2000, Celtic were looking enviously up at rivals Rangers, who had finished 21 points clear of the Hoops, to clinch the Scottish Premier League title...again.

That triumph was Rangers' eleventh in 12 years, a run broken by Celtic themselves in 1997/98, and the Parkhead club faithful were beginning to wonder if they were ever again going to be able to compete with their big-spending neighbours.

But then came Martin O'Neill, leaving the comfort zone of Leicester City to take what he described as his "dream job" of managing his boyhood heroes. And 12 months later second-best Celtic had pulled off a clean sweep of Scotland's major trophies.

Helped by a return to fitness of the remarkable goalscorer Henrik Larsson, and strengthened by the arrival of new signings such as £6m striker Chris Sutton and Belgian defender Joos Valgaeren, Celtic set a blistering pace.

The highlight of the season came early, with August's crushing 6-2 win over Rangers, a match that showed the whole of Scotland how far the Bhoys had come under O'Neill's inspirational brand of leadership.

Attracted by the side's style and success, further new signings soon arrived to help the cause. Midfielders Alan Thompson, from Aston Villa, and Leicester's Neil Lennon joined up, as did the former Tottenham defender Ramon Vega as Celtic embarked on an amazing run that saw them win 28 out of their first 33 games of the campaign.

"It's been phenomenal, as good as anything I've achieved in football," said a delighted Martin O'Neill after his side clinched the title with a scrappy 1-0 win over St. Mirren last April.

"At times it has seemed like the longest season of my life, though in some ways it seems only five minutes since August.

"Maybe the reason we won the title was because Rangers have not had such a clever season, but my old boss Brian Clough used to say that teams that win the Championship have usually been the best."

Next comes the challenge of Europe and a bid to stay in continental competition until after Christmas for the first time in more than 20 years.

"We have to strengthen the side for Europe," admits the former Irish international who made his managerial name at Leicester and Wycombe Wanderers. "We are not strong enough in a few areas, and that is something we need to address."

The secret to O'Neill's success has been the relationship he has managed to build up with the players at Parkhead, as midfield dynamo Jackie McNamara explains: "Last season was like a new start for everybody at Celtic," he says.

"All the players are of the same opinion. Martin O'Neill commands total respect in the dressing-room and we all want to do our best for him in every game."

Their best was certainly good enough in 2000/01.

FOOTBALL CRAZY!

It's time for another selection of mad but true tales from the fantastically odd world of football. Enjoy!

ENGLAND'S SHOOTING PRACTICE

In the winter of 1996 England played the former Soviet republic of Georgia in a World Cup qualifying game.

The players were a bit alarmed when they reached reception at the team hotel to be handed a notice saying: "You will be able to take your handguns into your rooms, but semi-automatic weapons must be left at reception."

Maybe they had heard that David Beckham had a good shot!

SNOW JOKE

It was a big surprise when Peterborough took on trial a 25-year-old Nigerian forward called Jesilimi Balogun a few years ago. While playing for the Reserves one afternoon it began to snow and Jesilimi, who had never seen snow before, was so freaked out that he ran off the pitch and refused to step back outside until the snow had stopped falling.

Although he never made the first-team at Posh, Jesilimi did go on to play League football with QPR.

HEADING FOR AN ACCIDENT

Back in the old days the Main Stand at Barnsley's Oakwell Stadium had a pair of swing doors which led out onto the pitch.

One of the players, keen to make a dramatic entrance in order to spook that day's opponents, often charged headlong through them... until one day a prank playing team-mate reversed the hinges and the player knocked himself stone cold unconscious!

KEEP IT CLEAN, DEAN

It was no laughing matter when striker Dean Windass got his marching orders while playing for Aberdeen a couple of years back.

Windass was dismissed THREE times in a match against Dundee Utd. Sent-off for a second bookable offence, Windass then hurled a volley of abuse at referee Stewart Dougal to earn himself a second red card.

His third offence was to rip out a corner flag and throw it to the ground on his way off the pitch. Windass went into the game with nine penalty points - and left it with 31!

KEEPER OR SWEEPER?

The thing with being a goalkeeper is that you spend a lot of time leaping around in muddy puddles pulling off spectacular saves, right? Wrong!

Spanish international 'keeper Zamora hated dirt and mess so much that he often took a broom out onto the field of play to sweep his goalmouth during quiet moments of the match!

YOU MUST BE JOACHIM

Legendary Brazilian striker Roberto Rivelino was famed for the power and accuracy of his shooting, and never was it better shown than when he was playing for Corinthians in a League match against Rio Preto.

As soon as the ref blew for kick-off, Rivelino looked up to see that the Rio Preto goalkeeper, Joachim Isadore, was still saying his pre-match prayers. So Rivelino simply blasted the ball over the goalie's head and in! Pick that one out.

Artwork: Barry Holmes, barry@meta-gb.com

ARSENAL

THE CLUB, NOW KNOWN AS ONE OF NORTH LONDON'S FINEST, WAS FOUNDED AT THE GOVERNMENT'S ROYAL ARSENAL ARMS FACTORY IN WOOLWICH, SOUTH LONDON, IN 1886. THEY STARTED PLAYING UNDER THE NAME OF DIAL SQUARE, ONE OF THE WORKSHOPS AT THE FACTORY.

GUNNERS

A reference to the club's birth in an arms factory

ODD SPOT

The Gunners believe that the ghost of a dead horse brings them luck! The unfortunate nag, which died in a construction accident during the building of Highbury, is buried under the site of what is now the North Bank.

HEROES

PAT JENNINGS (1977-84) Legendary Irish goalkeeper who joined from rivals Tottenham.

DAVID O'LEARY (1975-93) Current Leeds boss who played a record 722 games.

IAN WRIGHT (1991-98) Goalscoring phenomenon who notched up 185 goals for Arsenal after signing from Palace for £2.5m.

CURRENT STAR

THIERRY HENRY
A £10.5m signing from Juventus in August 1999, Henry has finished the last two seasons as Arsenal's leading scorer. Born in Paris, he was France's top scorer at World Cup 1998 and two years later again played a vital role as his country triumphed at Euro 2000.

FIRST SEASON

KIT →

FINISHED
9th in the 15-club Second Division 1893/94

FAMOUS FANS

Comedian Rory McGrath, who stars on TV quiz 'They Think It's All Over', is a regular at Highbury, as is talkSPORT radio's Tom Watt. Chart outfit Damage (pictured above) also follow the north London side.

COMPLETE LEAGUE RECORD

P	W	D	L	F	A
3878	1706	971	1201	6364	5037

ASTON VILLA

IN 1874 FOUR MEMBERS OF ASTON VILLA CRICKET CLUB DECIDED TO SET UP A FOOTBALL TEAM TO KEEP FIT DURING THE WINTER. THEIR FIRST MATCH WAS AGAINST A RUGBY SIDE, WITH THE FIRST-HALF PLAYED UNDER RUGBY RULES, THE SECOND FOOTBALL.

ASTON VILLA F.C.

PREPARED

THE VILLANS

Derived from the club's name

ODD SPOT

Villa have spent the grand total of 92 seasons in the top flight of English football. Only Everton, with 99, can boast more time at the pinnacle of the game.

HEROES

DAVID PLATT (1987-90) Former England captain who was voted PFA Player of the Year in 1990.

PAUL McGRATH (1989-93) Tough-tackling Irishman who was one of the finest central defenders of his era. Remains Villa's most capped player.

DWIGHT YORKE (1989-98) Quick and skilful striker who moved on to Man United for £12.6m in August 1998.

CURRENT STAR

GARETH BARRY
Widely considered to be one of the brightest young talents in the game, Gareth is still in his early 20s but already a regular in the England squad. Happy playing in the centre of defence or on the left side, he began with Brighton but was signed as a teenager by Villa.

FAMOUS FANS

Unfortunately for Villa fans, their most famous celebrity supporter is the wild-haired 'punk violinist' Kennedy!

FIRST SEASON

KIT →

FINISHED
Runners-up to Preston
1888

COMPLETE LEAGUE RECORD

P	W	D	L	F	A
4014	1699	926	1389	6692	5843

BLACKBURN

ARTE ET LABORE

A GROUP OF OLD BOYS FROM BLACKBURN GRAMMAR SCHOOL GOT TOGETHER TO FORM THE CLUB IN 1875, AND THEY WENT ON TO BECOME ONE OF THE FOUNDER MEMBERS OF THE FOOTBALL LEAGUE 13 YEARS LATER.

ROVERS

ODD SPOT

Alan Shearer is Rovers' most prolific scorer in recent times. The England ace netted an amazing 122 goals in 138 games for the club.

HEROES

ALAN SHEARER (1992-96) Became Britain's most expensive ever player when he joined Rovers from Saints for £3.6m in July 1992.

KEVIN DAVIES (1998-99) A whopping £7.25m took the England U21 star to Ewood Park from Southampton in June 1998.

LEE CARSLEY (1999-2000) A driving force in midfield, moved to Coventry last season.

CURRENT STAR

MATT JANSEN
One of the most exciting players outside the top flight last season, this left-sided striker looks set for a regular place in the England squad if he can repeat his form in the Premiership. Started with Carlisle and played for C. Palace before joining Rovers for £4m in January 1999.

FIRST SEASON

KIT →

FINISHED
4th in the first Football League season in 1888/89

FAMOUS FANS

Their most famous fan of all is Jack Walker (above right), the multi-millionaire businessman who bought the club and bankrolled their 1995 Premiership title win. Sadly, Walker died in the year 2000.

COMPLETE LEAGUE RECORD

P	W	D	L	F	A
4116	1631	1007	1478	6437	6115

BOLTON

BOYS FROM CHRIST CHURCH SUNDAY SCHOOL AND THEIR TEACHER, THOMAS OGDEN, FOUNDED A CLUB IN 1874. THE LOCAL VICAR BECAME CLUB PRESIDENT, BUT FOLLOWING A DISAGREEMENT, THE BOYS BROKE AWAY AND FORMED BOLTON WANDERERS IN 1877.

THE TROTTERS

In the 1880s the team were well known for their practical jokes - and a 'trotter' is a practical joker in Lancashire.

ODD SPOT

Early in their history Bolton tried a weird experiment to try and get more points. The Trotters started playing in white shirts with red spots because they thought it made their players look bigger and more scary!

HEROES

PETER REID (1974-82) Now manager at Sunderland, Reidy began his career as a tough-tackling midfielder with Wanderers.

JASON McATEER (1992-95) Began with Bolton before a £4.5m move to Liverpool. Helped Blackburn to promotion last season.

EIDUR GUDJOHNSEN (1998-2000) Skilful striker who is a regular international for Iceland. Joined Chelsea for £4m in 2000.

CURRENT STAR

MICHAEL RICKETTS
A surprise £400,000 signing from Walsall in the summer of 2000, this powerful youngster (pic right) went on to become Bolton's top scorer as the club roared back into the Premiership.

Eidur Gudjohnsen

FIRST SEASON

KIT →

FINISHED
5th in the first Football League season in 1888/89

FAMOUS FANS

Comedian Peter Kay and Emma Forbes, the former presenter of BBC1's Saturday morning kids' show 'Live and Kicking', both pin their colours to Bolton's mast.

COMPLETE LEAGUE RECORD

P	W	D	L	F	A
4150	1639	991	1520	6294	5950

CHARLTON

ADDICKS

or Robins or Valiants. Robins because of their red shirts, Valiants after their home stadium. In the old days the players changed above a fish and chip shop and the owner would turn up at home games waving a haddock nailed to a stick - this is said to be the origin of the club's Addicks nickname.

ODD SPOT

The site of what is now The Valley was a derelict chalk pit with a well. Some of the earth used in the construction of the stadium came from a local hospital - and was full of old bones!

HEROES

ALLAN SIMONSEN (1982) It doesn't seem so strange now, but it was amazing when Charlton signed this former European Footballer of the Year.

LEE BOWYER (1994-96) Leeds' star began at Charlton, before his £2.6m move.

ROB LEE (1983-92) A teenage turnstile operator at The Valley, Rob went on to play for Newcastle and England.

CURRENT STAR

MARK KINSELLA
After seven seasons at Colchester it looked like glory had passed by midfielder Mark. But Charlton splashed £150,000 on the player in September 1996 and he has become a Republic of Ireland regular and one of the stars of the Premiership.

FAMOUS FANS

The former boss of TV station Channel Four, Michael Grade, is a local lad and among the club's most loyal fans.

FIRST SEASON

KIT →

FINISHED
16th in the Third Division (South)
1921/22

COMPLETE LEAGUE RECORD

P	W	D	L	F	A
3100	1135	776	1189	4543	4762

CHELSEA

FORMED IN 1905 BY GUS MEARS, WHO WAS TEMPTED TO SELL THE LAND AT STAMFORD BRIDGE TO GREAT WESTERN RAILWAY FOR A COAL DUMPING YARD. BUT HE WAS PERSUADED BY A FRIEND CALLED FREDERICK PARKER TO USE THE LAND TO FORM A FOOTBALL CLUB.

THE BLUES

ODD SPOT

Chelsea's Stamford Bridge stadium remains the only ground in English football to be built before the creation of the team whose home it became.

HEROES

JIMMY GREAVES (1957-61) One of the greatest goalscorers of all time, Greavsie notched a club record 41 League goals way back in 1960/61.

GEORGE WEAH (2000) A one-time World, European and African Footballer of the Year, he helped guide Chelsea to the 2000 FA Cup.

TORE ANDRE FLO (1997-2000) Signed for £300,000 in August 1997 and twice top scored before joining Rangers in 2000.

CURRENT STAR

MARCEL DESAILLY
With World Cup and Euro Championship medals under his belt, Desailly is one of the world's most sought-after defenders. He joined Chelsea from AC Milan for £4.6m in July 1998 and has earned the nickname of 'The Rock'.

FAMOUS FANS

These days he lives in a house, a very big house, in the country. But Damon Albarn from Blur grew up watching Chelsea.

FIRST SEASON

KIT →

FINISHED
3rd in the Second Division
1905/06

COMPLETE LEAGUE RECORD

P	W	D	L	F	A
3500	1354	926	1220	5265	5054

DERBY COUNTY

DERBY

A GROUP OF PLAYERS FROM DERBYSHIRE COUNTY CRICKET CLUB THOUGHT THAT A FOOTBALL CLUB WOULD HELP BOOST THEIR FINANCES AND FORMED DERBY COUNTY IN 1884. THEY EVEN ADOPTED THE COLOURS OF THE CRICKET CLUB FOR THEIR FIRST PLAYING STRIP.

THE RAMS

Because the ram is the mascot of the nearby Sherwood Foresters' army Regiment.

ODD SPOT

Derby have played in 13 FA Cup Semi-Finals, yet have reached the Final just four times, winning the trophy only once. That victory came in 1946, after captain Jack Nicholas pleaded with local gypsies to lift a curse which had been placed on the club in 1895.

HEROES

DEAN SAUNDERS (1988-91) Welsh striker who became the club's record sale when he joined Liverpool for £2.9m in July 1991.

PETER SHILTON (1987-92) Won a record number of caps for England, 125, and was the greatest goalkeeper of his generation.

IGOR STIMAC (1997-99) Croatian defender (pic below) who became a big favourite with the Derby fans after joining the club in 1995.

CURRENT STAR

CRAIG BURLEY
The nephew of Ipswich manager George Burley, Craig is Derby's toothless midfielder who boasts a mega-bite in his tackles. A star for Scotland at international level, he likes to push forward and support his attack and has proved a bargain since his £3m move from Celtic in 1999.

FAMOUS FANS

Tracey Shaw - the actress who plays hairdresser Maxine in Coronation Street - cuts no corners with her love for Derby County.

FIRST SEASON

KIT →

FINISHED
10th in the 1888/89 campaign.
Founder members of the League

COMPLETE LEAGUE RECORD

P	W	D	L	F	A
4042	1591	974	1477	6372	6023

EVERTON

IN COMMON WITH A LOT OF CLUBS, EVERTON CAN THANK THE CHURCH FOR THEIR EXISTENCE. REGULARS AT THE ST. DOMINGO CHURCH SUNDAY SCHOOL FORMED THE CLUB IN 1878 AND A YEAR LATER CHANGED THE NAME TO EVERTON.

ODD SPOT

Today's squad numbers range from 1 to 35 and beyond, but Everton became the first team to wear the figures 1 to 11 when they stepped out for their 3-0 FA Cup Final win over Man City in 1933. City's players wore 12-22 in the experiment.

HEROES

GARY LINEKER (1985-86) One of England's greatest ever strikers, and now a famous TV star.

NEVILLE SOUTHALL (1981-98) Long-serving legend who made a club record 578 League appearances.

NICK BARMBY (1996-2000) England man who made a controversial £6m move to rivals Liverpool.

CURRENT STAR

DAVID WEIR
Described by Everton boss Walter Smith as the "best signing I ever made", the consistent Weir is a rock in central defence for the Toffees. A tough tackler who is calm on the ball, he joined from Hearts for £250,000 in February 1999.

FAMOUS FANS

BBC TV's Question of Sport captain and snooker star, John Parrott, is right on cue with his support for the Toffees.

THE TOFFEES

The club became associated with a local toffee-making company shortly after changing their name to Everton. The nickname has stuck ever since.

FIRST SEASON

KIT →

FINISHED
8th in the 1888/89 campaign.
Founder member of the League

COMPLETE LEAGUE RECORD

P	W	D	L	F	A
4002	1645	985	1372	6452	5682

FULHAM

FORMED BY CHURCHGOERS AS FULHAM ST. ANDREW'S CHURCH SUNDAY SCHOOL FC IN 1879.

THE COTTAGERS

After their home ground of Craven Cottage

ODD SPOT

It all seems a long time ago, now, but Fulham became the first club to pay a player the massive sum of £100 a week when they coughed up that figure for England man Johnny Haynes in 1961.

HEROES

GEORGE BEST (1976-77) Arguably the greatest British player of all time, Bestie was a Man United legend who also had a spell at Craven Cottage.

GEOFF HORSFIELD (1998-2000) Scored bags of goals to fire Fulham to the Division Two title, moving to Birmingham for £2m.

JOHN SALAKO (1998-99) Ex-England winger with lots of top flight experience.

CURRENT STAR

LOUIS SAHA
The Cottagers' leading scorer last season, with 27 League goals to his credit, this striker signed from French club Metz for a fee of £2.1m, having previously been at Newcastle on loan.

FAMOUS FANS

Club owner Mohamed Al Fayed has invited lots of famous faces to the Cottage in recent seasons, none more so than singing superstar Michael Jackson (below).

FIRST SEASON

KIT →

FINISHED
4th in the Second Division in the 1907/08 season

COMPLETE LEAGUE RECORD

P	W	D	L	F	A
3572	1366	891	1315	5314	5061

IPSWICH

FORMED AS IPSWICH ASSOCIATION FC IN 1878. TWO YEARS LATER THEY AMALGAMATED WITH IPSWICH FC, WHO PLAYED RUGBY, AND THE OVAL BALL GAME WAS DROPPED FIVE YEARS AFTER THAT.

IPSWICH TOWN FOOTBALL CLUB

ODD SPOT

Ipswich called in a witch doctor in the 1997/98 season to get rid of evil spirits they believed were haunting one of the goals at Portman Road!

HEROES

MICK MILLS (1965-82) Now assistant boss at Birmingham, Mills skippered the club to FA and UEFA Cup glory as well as making a record 591 League appearances.

JOHN WARK (1974-83, 1987-90, 1991-97) Three times a legend at Portman Road, Scotland international Wark (pic below) played in midfield and central defence.

KIERON DYER (1997-99) Town's record sale at £6m to Newcastle in July 1999.

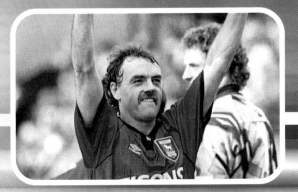

CURRENT STAR

MARCUS STEWART
Top scorer last season as Ipswich enjoyed a remarkable campaign on their return to the top flight. Town forked out £2.5m for Marcus' services in February 2000, but this intelligent and skilful striker has paid back that fee ten times over.

FIRST SEASON

KIT →

FINISHED
7th in the Third Division (South)
1938/39

FAMOUS FANS

Hannah from S Club 7 is the cousin of former Town star Eddie Spearitt and still follows Ipswich's fortunes.

TRACTOR BOYS

Also known as Town or Blues. It was only last season the supporters began referring to their side as the Tractor Boys, a joke about their reputation as 'country yokels'.

COMPLETE LEAGUE RECORD

P	W	D	L	F	A
2410	992	593	825	3605	3298

LEEDS

A LEEDS CITY CLUB WAS FOUNDED IN 1904, BUT AFTER ILLEGAL PAYMENTS WERE MADE TO PLAYERS THE CLUB WAS WOUND UP BY THE FA IN 1919. IMMEDIATELY AFTER, LEEDS UNITED WAS FOUNDED.

UNITED

They were known as 'The Peacocks' in their early days, after the original name of Elland Road - the Old Peacock Ground.

ODD SPOT

Leeds adopted their famous all-white playing strip in the 1960s, when legendary United manager Don Revie decided to copy the colours of mighty Real Madrid.

HEROES

GORDON STRACHAN (1989-95) Now Coventry boss, Strachan skippered Leeds to the 1992 League title.

ERIC CANTONA (1992) Went on to become a legend at Man United, too, but began his English career at Leeds.

JIMMY FLOYD HASSELBAINK (1997-99) Last season's Premiership top scorer with Chelsea, Jimmy had two hugely successful goalscoring years with Leeds.

CURRENT STAR

HARRY KEWELL
An Australia international and one of the finest attacking midfielders in world football. Named as the PFA 'Young Player of the Year' for the 1999/2000 campaign, he missed much of last season with an Achilles tendon injury.

FAMOUS FANS

Top artist bloke Damien Hirst is an Elland Road man, while Mel B (pic below) also cheers on her Yorkshire heroes.

FIRST SEASON

KIT →

FINISHED
14th in the Second Division.
1920/21

COMPLETE LEAGUE RECORD

P	W	D	L	F	A
3090	1289	806	995	4659	4062

LEICESTER

IN 1884, OLD BOYS FROM WYGGESTON SCHOOL FOUNDED THE CLUB AFTER A MEETING IN A HOUSE IN FOSSE WAY - HENCE THE CLUB'S ORIGINAL NAME, LEICESTER FOSSE.

ODD SPOT

City have reached the FA Cup Final on four occasions - 1949, 1961, 1963 and 1969 - but have yet to win the trophy. Just to rub salt into the wound, in 1969 they not only lost the Cup Final, but got relegated too!

HEROES

GARY LINEKER (1978-85) Scored 95 goals in 194 League games for the Foxes and made his England debut while still at Filbert Street.

STAN COLLYMORE (2000-01) Had a brief stay at Leicester, scoring a hat-trick on his home debut before moving to Bradford.

NEIL LENNON (1996-2000) N.Ireland international and battling midfielder who followed manager Martin O'Neill to Celtic.

CURRENT STAR

MUZZY IZZET
Born in East London, but a Turkey international thanks to his father, Muzzy began his career with Chelsea. He initially moved to Filbert Street on loan in March 1996 before making the move permanent a few weeks later in a £650,000 deal.

FAMOUS FANS

TV pundit and ex-City star Gary Lineker still follows the Foxes' fortunes.

THE FOXES

Leicestershire was world-famous for its fox hunting.

FIRST SEASON

KIT ➡

FINISHED
4th in the Second Division.
1894/95

COMPLETE LEAGUE RECORD

P	W	D	L	F	A
3898	1446	986	1466	5931	6050

LIVERPOOL

LIVERPOOL WAS FOUNDED WHEN EVERTON QUIT ANFIELD AFTER A BUST-UP WITH LANDLORD JOHN HOULDING. HE STARTED A NEW CLUB AT THE GROUND - AND EVEN TRIED TO CALL THEM EVERTON - BUT EVENTUALLY SETTLED ON THE NAME LIVERPOOL ASSOCIATION FC.

REDS

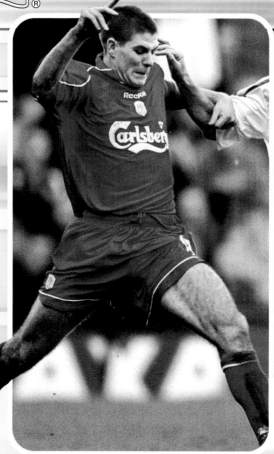

ODD SPOT

Man United have got a long way to go to beat Liverpool's impressive trophy-haul. The Reds have won the League title a record 18 times as well as four European Cups, three UEFA Cups, six FA Cups and six League Cups.

HEROES

KEVIN KEEGAN (1971-76) The former England boss was an Anfield legend in the 1970s, scoring goals and winning cups.

KENNY DALGLISH (1976-88) Brought in to replace Keegan, Dalglish won everything as a Reds' player and then led the side to the double in his first year as manager, in 1986.

STEVE McMANAMAN (1990-99) Winger who came up through the ranks at Anfield and now plays for Real Madrid.

CURRENT STAR

STEVEN GERRARD
If it was not for a persistent back injury, Steven would have won dozens of England caps by the time he was 20. A hard-working, tough-tackling midfielder with an eye for goal and good passing ability, he will be a star for years to come.

FIRST SEASON

KIT →

FINISHED
Champions of the Second Division 1893/94

FAMOUS FANS

Northern Star Melanie C is a huge Reds' fan and even used to be pictured in Liverpool kit while on Spice Girls duty.

COMPLETE LEAGUE RECORD

P	W	D	L	F	A
3878	1815	943	1120	6647	4905

MAN UTD

EMPLOYEES OF THE LANCASHIRE AND YORKSHIRE RAILWAY COMPANY FORMED NEWTON HEATH CRICKET AND FOOTBALL CLUB IN 1878. WHEN THE CLUB WENT BANKRUPT IN 1902, MANCHESTER UNITED WAS FOUNDED IN ITS PLACE.

RED DEVILS

ODD SPOT

With its all-seater capacity of 68,936 Old Trafford is comfortably the largest football stadium in the Premiership.

HEROES

GEORGE BEST (1963-73) European Footballer of the Year in 1968 when he helped United become the first English side to lift the European Cup.

BRYAN ROBSON (1981-1994) The driving force for club and country for many years and one of the world's best midfielders.

ERIC CANTONA (1992-97) Helped turn United from a good side into a great one, inspiring the club to four League titles.

CURRENT STAR

ROY KEANE
Signed from Nottingham Forest for a then record £3.75m in July 1993, Roy has gone on to become an Old Trafford legend. A regular in the Rep of Ireland side, he was voted the PFA and Football Writers' Footballer of the Year in 1999/2000.

FAMOUS FANS

Zoe Ball is live and kicking at Old Trafford, while TV funnyman Angus Deayton and chef Gary Rhodes are also United nuts.

FIRST SEASON

KIT →

FINISHED
bottom of the First Division
1892/93

COMPLETE LEAGUE RECORD

P	W	D	L	F	A
3910	1788	960	1162	6658	5156

MIDDLESBROUGH

LIKE SEVERAL OTHER CLUBS, MIDDLESBROUGH CAN THANK CRICKET FOR THEIR FOUNDATION. IT WAS MEMBERS OF THE MIDDLESBROUGH CRICKET CLUB WHO FORMED THE FOOTBALL TEAM FOLLOWING A MEETING IN THE GYMNASIUM OF THE CITY'S ALBERT PARK HOTEL IN 1875.

BORO

ODD SPOT

As the debate surrounding the new-look transfer system rages on, it is worth remembering that Boro were the first club to pay a four-figure sum to sign a player. In 1905 they tempted England star Alf Common from neighbours Sunderland for the princely sum of £1,000.

HEROES

TONY MOWBRAY (1981-91) Made more than 350 League appearances for the club before leaving for Celtic in a £1m transfer. Now first-team coach at Ipswich.

PAUL GASCOIGNE (1998-2000) The most exciting midfielder the English game has produced in the last 20 years.

JUNINHO (1995-97; 1999) Brazilian international (below) who was a huge favourite in two spells with the club.

CURRENT STAR

ALEN BOKSIC
Former Marseille, Lazio and Juventus striker who began last season with a burst of five goals in six games following his £2.5m arrival at the Riverside. He is an international for Croatia.

FAMOUS FANS

Chris Rea, actor Stephen Tompkinson from Ballykissangel and comedian Bob Mortimer are all Boro barmy.

FIRST SEASON

KIT →

FINISHED
14th in the Second Division
1899/00

COMPLETE LEAGUE RECORD

P	W	D	L	F	A
3744	1422	914	1408	5676	5495

NEWCASTLE

ORIGINALLY KNOWN AS STANLEY IN 1881, THE CLUB CHANGED THEIR NAME TO NEWCASTLE EAST END A YEAR LATER. IN 1889, NEWCASTLE WEST END, WHO PLAYED AT ST. JAMES' PARK, FOLDED AND INVITED THEIR RIVALS TO TAKE OVER THEIR GROUND, BECOMING NEWCASTLE UNITED.

NEWCASTLE UNITED

ODD SPOT

Facilities at St. James' Park were poor in the early days, with players changing in local pubs and butchers allowed to graze their sheep on the pitch!

HEROES

KEVIN KEEGAN (1982-84) A hero on Tyneside as a player and a manager - he got the club promoted in both jobs.

ANDY COLE (1993-95) Signed from Bristol City for £1.75m, Cole went on to score 55 goals in 70 League games for the club.

LEE CLARK (1989-97) Home grown star who came up through the ranks to shine in midfield before moving to Sunderland and Fulham.

CURRENT STAR

KIERON DYER
One of Ruud Gullit's last moves as Newcastle boss was to splash out £6m on Ipswich midfielder Dyer. Even at that price the England man looks a bargain. Quick, skilful and hard-working, Dyer's exciting, direct approach makes things happen for club and country.

FAMOUS FANS

TV presenters Ant (pic below with ex-Utd star Peter Beardsley) and Dec are fully tuned in members of the Toon Army.

FIRST SEASON

KIT →

FINISHED
4th in the Second Division
1893/94

THE MAGPIES

Legend has it that the nickname comes from the fact that a Dutch priest by the name of Father Dalmatives Houtmann was often seen talking to the players wearing a black and white cloak.

COMPLETE LEAGUE RECORD

P	W	D	L	F	A
3902	1608	904	1390	6231	5579

SOUTHAMPTON

MEMBERS OF THE YOUNG MEN'S ASSOCIATION OF ST. MARY'S CHURCH HELD A MEETING IN 1885 AND FORMED SOUTHAMPTON ST. MARY'S.

SAINTS

A reference to their foundation as a church side.

ODD SPOT

Saints moved into a new £30m stadium at the beginning of the 2001/02 season. It is situated in the St. Mary's area of the city, where they first played 115 years ago.

CURRENT STAR

JAMES BEATTIE
James was on the verge of being sold to Crystal Palace early last season, but he hit back with a great spell of 10 goals in 10 games and went on to establish himself as a key member of the side.

FAMOUS FANS

Singing sensation Craig David is a big Saints follower, as are fellow hit chart act Artful Dodger.

HEROES

ALAN SHEARER (1988-92) Ex-England captain who began at The Dell and scored a hat-trick on his debut, against Arsenal.

TIM FLOWERS (1986-93) Goalkeeper Tim (pic below) played more than 240 games for Saints before leaving to win the League with Blackburn in 1995. Now with Leicester.

LUIS BOA MORTE (1999-2000) Began his English career at Arsenal before joining Saints in August 1999. Helped Fulham to the Division One title last season.

FIRST SEASON

KIT →

FINISHED
Runners-up in Third Division (South)
1920/21

COMPLETE LEAGUE RECORD

P	W	D	L	F	A
3098	1173	794	1131	4667	4532

SUNDERLAND

FORMED BY A GROUP OF TEACHERS, LED BY A MAN CALLED JAMES ALLAN, IN 1879 AT THE ADULTS SCHOOL IN NORFOLK STREET. DUE TO FINANCIAL PROBLEMS, IT WAS QUICKLY AGREED TO INCLUDE PEOPLE FROM OUTSIDE THE TEACHING PROFESSION.

CONSECTATIO EXCELLENTIAE

SUNDERLAND A.F.C.

ODD SPOT

Peter Reid is quite a rarity at Sunderland - he's English! It took the club 60 years before they appointed an English boss, with Alan Brown taking over in 1957.

HEROES

MARCO GABBIADINI (1987-91) Double 'Golden Boot' winner who first hit the big time with Sunderland and went on to win England 'B' caps.

MICHAEL BRIDGES (1995-99) Skilful young homegrown striker who became the club's record sale when he joined Leeds for £5.6m in July 1999.

CHRIS MAKIN (1997-2001) Can play on either flank and has picked up England honours at schools, youth and U21 levels. Joined Ipswich last season.

CURRENT STAR

KEVIN PHILLIPS
The £325,000 that Sunderland paid Watford for Phillips in July 1997 must go down as one of the biggest bargains of all time. Strong and quick, he has gone on to play for England and is one of the most dangerous strikers in the Premiership.

FAMOUS FANS

Former Olympic and World Champion middle distance runner, Steve Cram (number 343 in pic below).

FIRST SEASON

KIT →

FINISHED
7th in the Football League 1890/91

THE BLACK CATS

Adopted in 1999/2000 following a vote by supporters. Previously the side were known as the Rokermen, after their former ground at Roker Park.

COMPLETE LEAGUE RECORD

P	W	D	L	F	A
4020	1653	980	1387	6444	5763

TOTTENHAM

A GROUP OF OLD BOYS FROM ST. JOHN'S PRESBYTERIAN AND TOTTENHAM GRAMMAR SCHOOL GOT TOGETHER TO FORM HOTSPUR FC IN 1882, HOLDING MEETINGS IN THE RED HOUSE ON TOTTENHAM HIGH ROAD. THE BUILDING STILL HOUSES THE CLUB'S OFFICES TODAY.

SPURS

ODD SPOT

In 1889 Spurs changed their playing strip from all blue to their current colours of white shirts and navy blue shorts. It was a tribute to Preston North End, the most successful team of that era.

HEROES

GLENN HODDLE (1974-87) Spurs legend who returned to the club as manager in March 2001.

PAUL GASCOIGNE (1988-92) The most naturally gifted player to grace the English game in the last 20 years.

TEDDY SHERINGHAM (1992-97) The Footballer of the Year has returned for a second spell at Spurs this season.

CURRENT STAR

STEPHEN CARR
A Republic of Ireland international who has come up through the ranks at White Hart Lane to become a regular at right-back. Quick and strong, he also possesses a powerful shot and scored some spectacular goals last season.

FIRST SEASON

KIT →

FINISHED
Runners-up in the Second Division
1908/09

FAMOUS FANS

There must be some rows in the Bunton household - Baby Spice Emma loves Spurs, while boyfriend Jade is an Arsenal man!

COMPLETE LEAGUE RECORD

P	W	D	L	F	A
3378	1397	835	1146	5534	4760

AUDERE·EST·FACERE

WEST HAM

EMPLOYEES OF A LOCAL SHIP-BUILDING YARD AT THAMES IRONWORKS FORMED THAMES IRONWORKS FC IN 1895. FINANCIAL PROBLEMS RESULTED IN ITS CLOSURE IN JUNE 1900, BUT IT WAS RELAUNCHED A MONTH LATER AS WEST HAM UNITED FC.

ODD SPOT

Back in 1980 West Ham became the last club from outside the top flight to win the FA Cup. The Hammers - then in the old Division Two - beat Arsenal 1-0 in the Final thanks to a rare headed goal by Trevor Brooking.

HEROES

PAUL INCE (1985-1989) England midfielder who began at West Ham. Moved on to Man United, Inter Milan and Liverpool and is currently battling away for Middlesbrough.

PAULO WANCHOPE (1999-2000) Costa Rica international who is capable of scoring the most spectacular goals with his unpredictable skills. Joined Man City last season.

RIO FERDINAND (1995-2000) Came up through the junior sides to become a first-team regular. Now at Leeds.

CURRENT STAR

MICHAEL CARRICK
Another exciting prospect to graduate from the West Ham youth academy, Michael is firmly established in the Hammers' midfield. A tough tackler, he normally plays just in front of the defence. Born in the North East, he was a Newcastle fan as a youngster.

FAMOUS FANS

West Ham make actor Nick Berry's heart beat, while comic Phill Jupitus is also a fan.

THE HAMMERS

Also known as the Irons. Hammers symbolize the tools of a ship-yard worker

FIRST SEASON

KIT →

FINISHED
7th in the Second Division
1919/20

COMPLETE LEAGUE RECORD

P	W	D	L	F	A
3132	1193	772	1167	4759	4655

CELTIC

FORMED IN 1887 BY IRISH CATHOLICS AS A CHARITY, WITH THE MAIN AIM OF PROVIDING SOUP KITCHENS FOR THE POOR OF GLASGOW'S EAST END.

THE BHOYS

The closest English spelling to the Gaelic word for 'boys'

ODD SPOT

Celtic's famous stadium is nicknamed 'Paradise' by fans because when the club moved from the original Celtic Park in 1892 one onlooker remarked: "It's like leaving a graveyard to enter paradise".

HEROES

KENNY DALGLISH (1970-77) Celtic's number one living legend - despite being a mad-keen Rangers fan as a boy.

PAOLO DI CANIO (1996-97) One of the most exciting players in Britain, Paolo (below) was Scotland's Player of the Year.

MARK VIDUKA (1999-2000) 25 League goals in his first season with Celtic before a big money move to Leeds.

CURRENT STAR

HENRIK LARSSON
The Swedish international's remarkable goal return of 35 goals last season took the League title to Celtic Park for only the second time in the last 13 years. Snapped up from Dutch giants Feyenoord prior to the 1997/98 campaign - when he again top scored as the Bhoys won the title.

FAMOUS FANS

Silky-voiced Texas singer Charlene Spiteri can be seen roaring on The Bhoys at Celtic Park.

FIRST SEASON

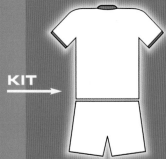

KIT →

FINISHED
Celtic finished third in the first Scottish League season in 1890/91.

LAST SEASON'S LEAGUE RECORD

P	W	D	L	F	A
36	31	4	1	90	26

RANGERS

A GROUP OF OARSMEN FROM CLYDE, LOOKING FOR A WINTER PASTIME, FOUNDED THE CLUB IN 1873. THEY TOOK THEIR NAME FROM AN ENGLISH RUGBY CLUB OF THE TIME.

A shortening of the club's name

THE GERS

ODD SPOT

The first ever game between Rangers and Celtic was a friendly in every sense of the word. After Celtic's 5-2 win in May 1888, the players went off for a supper and celebration together at a local hall. Can't imagine that happening these days!

HEROES

ALLY McCOIST (1983-98) Rangers' all-time greatest scorer, Ally (below) hit 355 goals during 15 years at the club.

GRAEME SOUNESS (1986) The man who made Rangers great again. Led the club to League titles and cups galore.

ANDREI KANCHELSKIS (1998-2001) Skilful and lightning fast, he's also played for Man United, Everton and Fiorentina.

CURRENT STAR

TORE ANDRE FLO
When you are a big money striker, scoring a goal on your debut is always a great way to arrive. Doing it in a 5-1 thrashing of your biggest rivals goes one step further. Flo managed both following his £12m transfer from Chelsea in November 2000.

FAMOUS FANS

Sean Connery, the original James Bond, proved to be a double agent, ditching Celtic for Rangers in recent years.

FIRST SEASON

KIT →

FINISHED
Rangers shared the first Scottish League title with Dumbarton in 1890/91.

LAST SEASON'S LEAGUE RECORD

P	W	D	L	F	A
36	24	4	8	67	35

HENRY THE FIRST

World class! There is no other description for Thierry Henry, Arsenal's World Cup and European Championship winning superstar. Arsene Wenger knew exactly what he was getting when he paid £10.5m to Juventus for him in the summer of 1999 but then he would, he had been his boss a few years earlier at Monaco.

THIERRY HENRY began life on August 17th 1977 in Les Ulysses, Paris. Rugby was very popular in the area, and could easily have been his sport. But the young Thierry chose football instead and starred in schools soccer, often playing against boys a year or two older than himself.

Despite his obvious talents, it was far-away Monaco who were the first to recognise Henry's potential. They offered him a place while he was in his early teens and at the age of 17 Arsene Wenger - now his manager at Arsenal - gave him his first-team debut on August 31st 1994 against Nice, after the youngster had struck 45 goals for the club's youth team the previous year. Henry's side lost 0-2 but he remained in the senior squad and towards the end of the season he was given more chances, starting two games, coming on as sub in six and hitting three important goals. His career as a top level goalscorer was underway and it has taken him all the way to the top of the world game.

Thierry captained the French national under-18s in 1996 and was voted French Young Footballer of the Year for his contribution to club and country. The following year he made his senior debut for France, on October 11th 1997, in a 2-1 win over South Africa in Lens. He was only just 20 years-old and quickly became the talk of France. "I was amazed to be called up for France when I was so young," admits Thierry. "But it was also a great honour and one I am still very proud to have."

Henry celebrates with first club Monaco

69

AS the 1998 World Cup approached, Aime Jacquet, the French national coach, decided to include Thierry Henry in his squad. It turned out to be a wise move as speedy Thierry scored three goals and helped France to win the World Cup on home territory. He was his country's top scorer in the tournament and won praise from Ronaldo. "I knew Henry was good, but I had no idea he was that good," said the Brazilian superstar.

JUVENTUS were trying to strengthen their squad in 1998/99 and after a few early games for Monaco, Henry found himself on the way to Italy. Having scored 20 goals in 105 League games for Monaco, Thierry found it difficult to settle in Italy but notched three goals in 16 matches before Arsenal swooped in 1999.

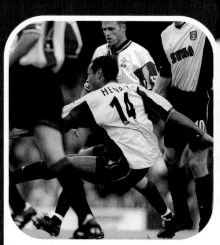

HE was Player of the Year as Arsenal reached the Final of the UEFA Cup, but they were beaten by Galatasaray. As League runners-up and UEFA Cup finalists the Gunners still had a pretty good season.

HIS former Monaco boss, Arsene Wenger, welcomed him to London with open arms. Thierry knew he had arrived when he hit the winner against Southampton on September 18th 1999, his first strike for the Gunners. "It was so hard at the beginning," he recalls. "I missed so many chances. But it eventually came good for me."

QUIZ QUESTION

THIERRY'S FIRST LEAGUE GAME FOR ARSENAL WAS A 2-1 WIN ON AUGUST 7TH 1999. WAS IT AGAINST LEICESTER, DERBY OR NEWCASTLE? ANSWER AT BOTTOM OF PAGE.

IT was not good enough for Thierry Henry, though. "I would be much happier if I did not get as many goals for the season but we won the Champions' League or the Premiership instead," insisted the French hitman. "My big target is to win a trophy or a title with Arsenal. That is the most pressing thing right now."

HIS form during the 2000/2001 season was second to none and once again Arsenal were in the hunt for all the major honours. At the end of the season they finished empty-handed, but Thierry Henry once again emerged as the hero of the Gunners' campaign, especially for some great goals and a memorable hat-trick on Boxing Day in a 6-1 win over Leicester. Arsene Wenger described him simply as 'a fantastic player' and if the Arsenal manager says that, who could argue?

HENRY SIDELINES

THIERRY SHUNS THE GLITZY CLUBBING NIGHTS OF MANY TOP SOCCER STARS BECAUSE HE LIKES A QUIET LIFE WITH HIS FAMILY.

HIS FAVOURITE OTHER SPORTS ARE RUGBY AND FORMULA ONE.

NOT SURPRISINGLY, HE LIKES FRENCH RESTAURANTS BUT IS NOT SO KEEN ON GOOD OLD ENGLISH FISH AND CHIPS. HIS ABSOLUTE FAVOURITE FOOD, HOWEVER, IS HIS MOTHER'S CARIBBEAN COOKING FROM HER HOME COUNTRY OF GUADALOUPE.

HENRY SAYS HE IS HAPPY AT ARSENAL BUT WOULD LIKE TO PLAY IN FRANCE AGAIN LATER IN HIS CAREER.

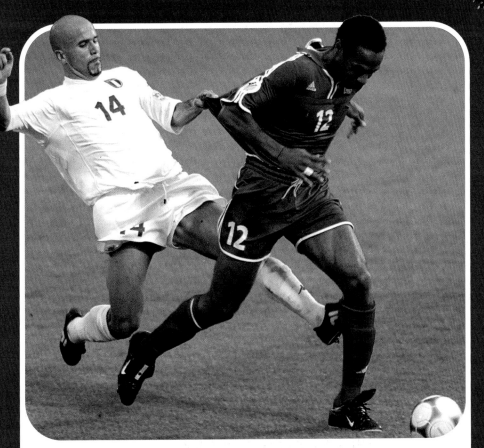

THIERRY resolved to do better in the European Championship during the summer of 2000 - and he certainly did. France won the tournament, Thierry was brilliant throughout and was even named Man of the Match in the Final in which France beat Italy 2-1. "It was great to win the Euro 2000 tournament with my country, because I was so disappointed not to have picked up any trophies at Arsenal that season," confirms Henry. "We were second in the Championship and runners-up in the UEFA Cup, but for us that was a big blow. I may already have won the two most important cups in the world, but now I have to work with my own club and concentrate on picking up some silverware for our fans."

Quiz answer: Leicester

71

UPS & DOWNS
WHAT IT'S BEEN LIKE TO FOLLOW FULHAM RECENTLY

	91/92*	92/93	93/94	94/95	95/96	96/97	97/98	98/99	99/00	00/01
DIV 1									9th	1st (P)
2	12th	21st (R)					6th	1st (P)		
3	9th			8th	17th	2nd (P)				

SEASON

(* denotes: league restructured, with Div 1 becoming the Premiership, Div 2 becoming Div 1 etc)

COTTAGE INDUSTRY

After a gap of 33 years, Fulham have returned to the top flight, having survived merger threats, possible ground closure and gone to the brink of relegation out of the Football League. Not surprisingly, they are delighted to be back.

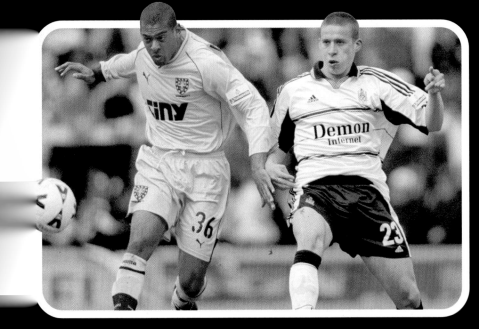

FULHAM'S high profile owner Mohamed Al Fayed caused a major stir when he tempted former Monaco boss Jean Tigana to take over the reins at Craven Cottage in July 2000.

Tigana was widely regarded as one of the brightest young coaching talents around, so what was he doing taking charge at a lower level English club with a history of underachievement?

It was all part of Al Fayed's ambitious scheme to turn the Cottagers into one of the country's leading clubs - and so far things are running pretty much to plan.

Fulham finished last season with a whopping 101 points to their credit, ten clear of second placed Blackburn. And they won admirers right across the country with the quality of their football.

According to midfielder Sean Davis (pictured above), the only regular first-team member last season to have come up through the ranks at Craven Cottage, the secret to their success is simple.

"Jean Tigana didn't put us under any pressure," explains Davis. "He just told us to go out there, enjoy ourselves and play entertaining football.

"We got off to a great start, which helped, and went 13 games unbeaten which gave us a good base to build from."

The Premiership holds no fears for Fulham, who have spent millions of pounds attracting experienced, top class players to west London over recent years.

The likes of John Collins (Scotland), Chris Coleman (Wales), Andy Melville

(Wales), Karlheinz Riedle (Germany) and Bjarne Goldbaek (Denmark) are all established internationals, while there is no shortage of cash left to bring in new faces as and when they are needed.

So are Fulham likely to 'do an Ipswich' and take the top flight by storm - or will it be a case of following Manchester City's example and dropping straight back through the relegation trapdoor?

Sean Davis, for one, has no doubts. "Ipswich play a similar style of passing game to us, and they did brilliantly and played some great football too," he explains. "There are an awful lot of players here with Premiership experience, so hopefully we can go on and achieve the same as Ipswich last year."

PART THREE

WHO WANTS TO BE A FOOTY-AIRE?

The competition is starting to hot up now, with the big prizes coming thick and fast. Have you used your lifelines yet? Keep going, you're nearly there! Turn to page 103 for the final set of questions.

12

9 Win: Qualify for Europe
Q. Which club has won the League title the most times?

- A. Manchester United
- B. Arsenal
- C. Leeds
- D. Liverpool

10 Win: Premiership title
Q. For which country is Leicester's Muzzy Izzet an international?

- A. Turkey
- B. England
- C. Republic of Ireland
- D. Malta

11 Win: European Player of the Year
Q. Who scored England's first goal in the 1998 World Cup finals?

- A. Alan Shearer
- B. Paul Scholes
- C. David Beckham
- D. Michael Owen

12 Win: The UEFA Cup
Q. For which Premiership club did Jermaine Wright play last season?

- A. Bradford
- B. Ipswich
- C. Coventry
- D. Charlton

Answers on page 110-111

QUESTION 9
PHONE THE COACH: d
SUB: Answers a and d are left.
ASK THE CROWD
A B C D

QUESTION 10
PHONE THE COACH: c
SUB: Answers a and c are left.
ASK THE CROWD
A B C D

QUESTION 11
PHONE THE COACH: a
SUB: Answers a and b are left.
ASK THE CROWD
A B C D

QUESTION 12
PHONE THE COACH: c
SUB: Answers b and c are left.
ASK THE CROWD
A B C D

LINK 'EM UP

CAN YOU JOIN THE CLUB NAMES AND GROUNDS TO THE CORRECT BADGES? WE'VE DONE THE FIRST ONE TO GET YOU GOING.

LIVERPOOL

FULHAM

BLACKBURN

TOTTENHAM

WEST HAM

IPSWICH

UPTON PARK

WHITE HART LANE

ANFIELD

PORTMAN ROAD

CRAVEN COTTAGE

EWOOD PARK

GRID WORD

IT'S TIME TO TEST YOUR FOOTBALL KNOWLEDGE. SIMPLY WRITE THE ANSWER TO EACH CLUE IN THE SPACES PROVIDED - ONCE YOU'VE GOT THEM ALL YOU WILL BE ABLE TO DECIPHER THE VITAL MESSAGE...AND WE'RE SURE YOU WILL AGREE! GOOD LUCK!

CLUES

1. Bolton reached the Premiership via these.
2. Where Charlton play their home games.
3. Name the English team that won all three cup competitions they entered last season.
4. Brighton were champions of which league last season?
5. Steve Bruce was appointed manager of which Division One side in the summer of 2001?
6. Voted Footballer of the Year last season.
7. Name the player who top scored in the Scottish League in 2000/01.
8. Leeds' manager is called...
9. Current Champions' League holders?
10. Luke Chadwick plays for which club?

1.
2.
3.
4.
5.
6.
7.
8.
9.
10.

WARP FACTOR

D'oh! It all went wrong when Shoot's tired designer accidentally hit the button marked "make all the pictures go weird". So now we need your help to identify the nine characters below so we can put them back in their rightful places. There's a clue for each one, just to set you on your way!

A
This striker is a Wizard of Oz at Elland Road.

B
Anfield ace who sounds a bit pesky!

C
Tractor Boy who ploughed through defences last year.

D
Chelsea favourite who is not going back to Serie A.

E
England midfield dynamo from Merseyside.

F
He's gone from talk of the Town to talk of the Toon.

G
Geordie born midfielder at Upton Park.

H
Top Bhoy who finished last season with golden boots.

I
Great Dane at The Valley.

Quiz Answers on pp110/111

THE HIT MEN

They are the players that keep the nets bulging and the headlines coming. Every club has its top striker, but these are the scoring sensations who set the Leagues alight with their goal-den touch last season.

JIMMY FLOYD HASSELBAINK CHELSEA

SIGNED for a whopping great £15m from Atletico Madrid in the summer of 2000, Jimmy was the star of Chelsea's disappointing season.

He started as he meant to go on, taking just 22 minutes of his first game for the Blues - the Charity Shield against Man United - to open his goal account with a powerful shot that took a deflection off Jaap Stam to deceive Fabien Barthez.

Gianluca Vialli was still in charge at Stamford Bridge at that time, and he was convinced that, even at £15m, he had found himself a bargain.

"He is a proven goalscorer and when you are a striker and scoring regularly, the confidence between you and your team-mates grows.

"They know they can give you the ball as often as they like because you can score.

"I am confident he will score as many goals as he did in Madrid."

And score goals Jimmy certainly did, even as his side struggled to come to terms with the sacking of the popular Vialli midway through the campaign, and his replacement by fellow Italian Claudio Ranieri.

The Dutch master went on to net 23 times in the League, the first Chelsea player to get above the 'teens' since Kerry Dixon hit 20 way back in the 1989/90 season.

But, although he was pleased to pick up the Golden Boot for his efforts, Hasselbaink - once with Leeds - was more concerned with a lack of trophies on his return to English football.

"I was glad to win the Golden Boot, of course I was, it would be silly to say

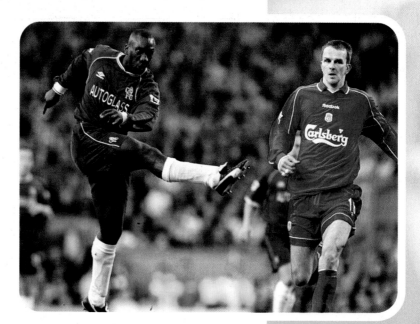

otherwise," explains the 29 year-old Holland international. "But it is this season that I am really thinking about now.

"It was quite a hard year for us, not one of the best for Chelsea. But getting into Europe was important and I am pleased that we achieved that."

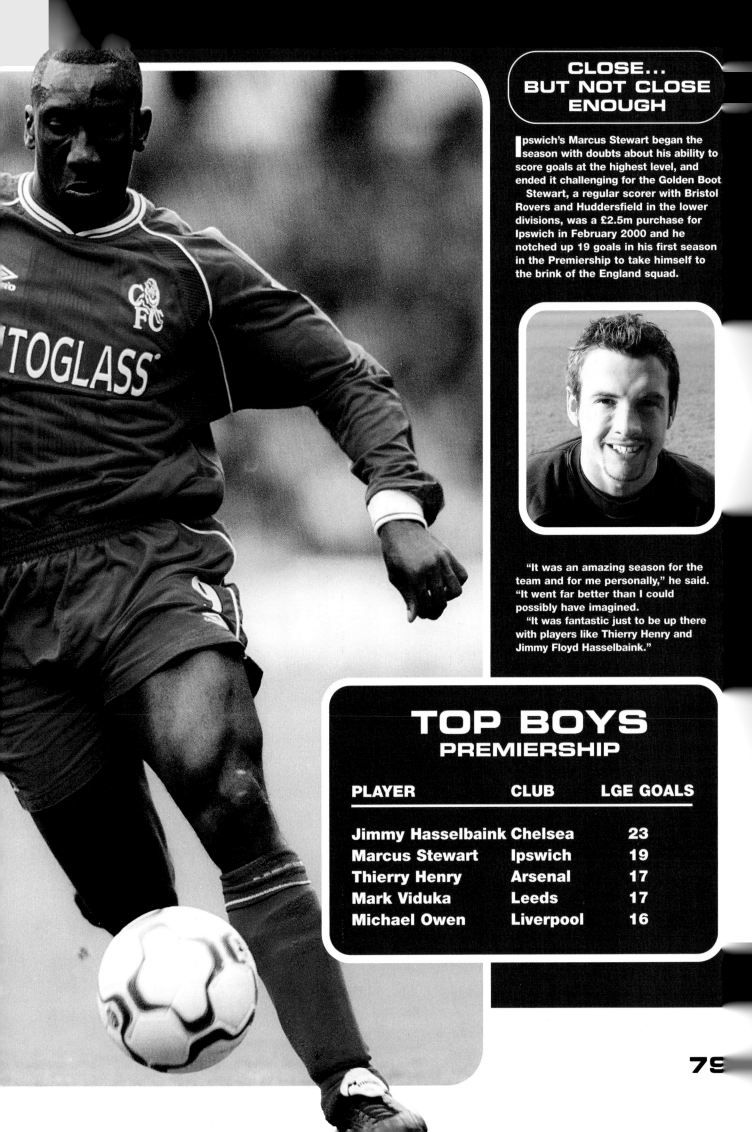

Ipswich's Marcus Stewart began the season with doubts about his ability to score goals at the highest level, and ended it challenging for the Golden Boot Stewart, a regular scorer with Bristol Rovers and Huddersfield in the lower divisions, was a £2.5m purchase for Ipswich in February 2000 and he notched up 19 goals in his first season in the Premiership to take himself to the brink of the England squad.

"It was an amazing season for the team and for me personally," he said. "It went far better than I could possibly have imagined.
   "It was fantastic just to be up there with players like Thierry Henry and Jimmy Floyd Hasselbaink."

TOP BOYS
PREMIERSHIP

PLAYER	CLUB	LGE GOALS
Jimmy Hasselbaink	Chelsea	23
Marcus Stewart	Ipswich	19
Thierry Henry	Arsenal	17
Mark Viduka	Leeds	17
Michael Owen	Liverpool	16

79

HENRIK LARSSON
CELTIC

THERE was no more remarkable striker in the whole of Europe last season then Celtic's amazing Henrik Larsson.

Having missed most of the previous campaign with a badly broken leg that at one stage looked likely to end his career, Larsson simply oozed class as he thumped home an amazing 53 goals - with 35 of those coming in the League campaign!

Add to that a further five goals scored for his country, Sweden, and you get a picture of a striker who was bang in form. He scored more than twice as many league goals as his nearest challenger in the Scottish Premiership.

Celtic's previous post-war scoring record - in all competitions - was 48 goals from Charlie Nicholas in 1982/83, while club legend Jimmy McGrory notched an incredible 50 League goals in the 1935/36 campaign.

All in all it has been a fantastic return for the £650,000 Celtic paid Dutch club Feyenoord for Larsson's signature in 1997.

Former Celtic and Man United star Brian McClair certainly believes that Larsson is an ideal front man. "He's fantastic - strong, quick and good with his head, too," he explains.

"It says a lot about him that he has achieved all this after coming back from a horrific injury. He obviously enjoys what he is doing, he is always smiling."

TOP BOYS
SCOTTISH PREMIERSHIP

PLAYER	CLUB	LGE GOALS
Henrik Larsson	Celtic	35
Arild Stavrum	Aberdeen	17
Juan Sara	Dundee	15
Tore Andre Flo	Rangers	14*
Andrew Kirk	Hearts	13

(* denotes: including three for Chelsea)

LOUIS SAHA
FULHAM

IT is little surprise that last season's runaway Division One Champions Fulham also boasted the services of the table's leading League scorer.

A £2.1m signing from French club Metz in July 2000, Louis Saha had previously had a spell on loan at Newcastle United, where he picked up some tips from ex-England skipper Alan Shearer on how to handle the game in this country.

"Playing at Newcastle was a great experience for me," he explains. "Alan Shearer gave me advice on passing and movement all the time. He told me I was very quick and that I should play fast all the time, which I try to do.

"But I knew I could score quite a lot of goals - I have proved it before in France.

"I thought it would take me a little longer to settle, I have been surprised how quickly I adapted to the English game."

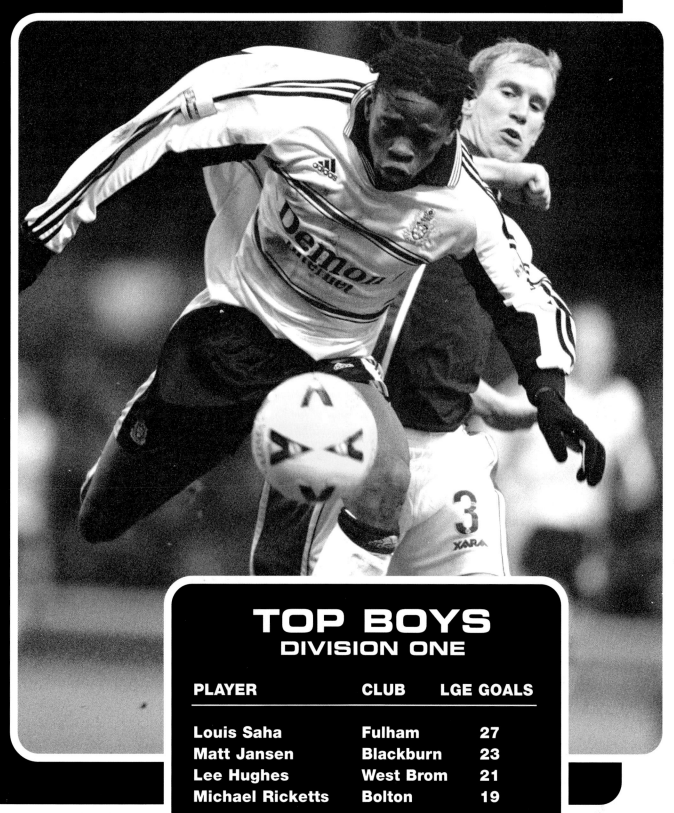

TOP BOYS
DIVISION ONE

PLAYER	CLUB	LGE GOALS
Louis Saha	Fulham	27
Matt Jansen	Blackburn	23
Lee Hughes	West Brom	21
Michael Ricketts	Bolton	19

TEDDY SHERINGHAM & GLENN HODDLE
TOTTENHAM

WHITE HART GAIN

Spurs fans were delighted to see Glenn Hoddle return to White Hart Lane as manager. After years in the shadow of neighbours Arsenal, could Tottenham finally be on the way back?

Ten years ago, Tottenham were rightly considered as one of English football's 'big five'. One of only a handful of clubs to have achieved the 'double' they have a roll of honour that boasts League titles, FA Cups, League Cups and European trophies.

Since the early 1990s, though, the club has slipped from that lofty perch and seen sides such as Leeds and Newcastle leapfrog above them into the positions of power.

And just to add insult to injury, bitter rivals Arsenal have enjoyed a decade of glory.

But it looks like the situation could be improving for Spurs. Under former boss George Graham Tottenham won their first trophy for eight years when they picked up the League Cup in 1999.

And with the signing of players such as Sergei Rebrov, from Dynamo Kiev, and the highly-rated Peterborough pair Matthew Etherington and Simon Davies, the foundations were put into place for further success.

When White Hart Lane legend Glenn Hoddle took over as boss in April 2001 he inherited a decent, but under-performing, squad and promptly set about strengthening it with the summer signings of Footballer of the Year Teddy Sheringham, from Man United, and Chelsea midfielder Gus Poyet.

Added to international performers such as Stephen Carr and Les Ferdinand, and promising youngsters like Luke Young, Alton Thelwell and Ledley King, the future looks bright for Tottenham.

Hoddle is delighted to be back at the club where he found fame and fortune as a brilliant midfield playmaker in the 1970s and 1980s.

"I feel very much at home here," he explains. "I first walked through the turnstiles when I was eight years of age.

"I left when I was 29. That is a massive part of my football career.

"It's emotional and exciting, a feeling of coming home.

"I have a deep-rooted feeling for Tottenham. It has always been my club. I know the feeling here, what the fans want and what they don't.

"I understand that and that is an advantage as we look to take the club forward."

The arrival of Poyet and Sheringham underlines Hoddle's plan to use experienced winners to help bring on his promising youngsters.

"We've got some terrific young players," says the ex-England coach. "But they need guidance.

"The ingredients we're missing are experience and knowing how to win.

"Both Teddy and Gus will bring our youngsters on in leaps and bounds.

"People talk about their age, but you've only got to look at what a 37 year-old Gary McAllister did for Liverpool last season to see how they can benefit us."

Spurs' fans hope that a man they once viewed as a footballing 'God' can help lead the club back into the promised land. Whisper it quietly, but he might just manage it.

SPURS' NUMBER ONES

They say that Spurs are most likely to win trophies when the year ends in a '1'. It's easy to see why...

League Champions
1951, 1961

Division Two Title
1920, 1950

FA Cup Winners
1901, 1921, 1961, 1962, 1967, 1981, 1982, 1991

League Cup Winners
1971, 1973, 1999

European Cup-Winners' Cup Winners
1963

UEFA Cup Winners
1972, 1984

Sergei Rebrov (left) will be hoping to help Tottenham emerge from Arsenal's shadow this season

HARRY HOTTER

Leeds United nearly went all the way to the Champions' League Final last season and their adventure earned them an army of new supporters. Star of the Leeds show is Harry Kewell.

NOT many people would have thought that little Harry would one day become a world soccer star when he was born in Smithfield on the outskirts of Sydney, Australia, on September 22nd 1978. With rugby, Aussie rules, hockey, swimming, tennis and cricket all taking priority over soccer, nobody would have given a thought to Harry's chances of even playing soccer let alone being any good at it. But when his older brother started banging a ball about in the back yard, Harry couldn't resist having a go as well.

Kewell was soon snapped up by the local under-6s side and it wasn't long before he became a member of the Australian Academy of Sport. The Aussie youth side travelled to South America and Asia for international matches and that is where he gained his first youth caps.

When the chance to move to England for a trial period with Leeds presented itself Harry was on the first available plane. He was only 16 when he arrived at Elland Road, but quickly settled in and played for the Leeds youth side, including the one which won the FA Youth Cup in 1997.

But much had happened before then. On December 23rd 1995 Leeds decided they had seen enough of the youngster and officially signed Harry from the Aussie Academy. He was 17-years-old and had started the season playing in the Northern Intermediate League. By the end of the campaign his world had changed dramatically. He made his senior debut for Leeds on March 30th 1996 in a 1-0 defeat by Middlesbrough.

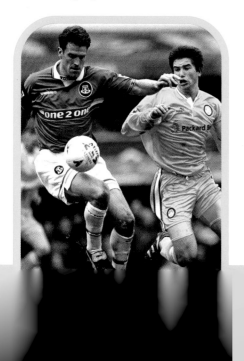

KEWELL was also gaining experience in international football and was called up for the Australian under-20 side for a tournament in Tahiti. He made his mark and was soon added to the senior squad. His debut was against Chile on April 23rd 1996. Chile won 3-0.

THE following season Harry spent most of his time learning his trade in the Leeds youth side, although he did play one Premiership game, against Tottenham. But it was in the 1997/98 season that Harry really came of age, with regular appearances and his first senior goal, on October 18th 1997, in a 4-1 win against Newcastle.

BY the end of the 1999/2000 season, in which Leeds finished third in the Premiership, he had missed only two League games and scored ten goals. His performances were terrific throughout the season and nobody was surprised when he was named Young Player of the Year by his fellow pros, as well as picking up the Leeds' club Player of the Year award. "We've grown up together as a team and we know what we are all about and how to play each week," said Harry. "It's good to have that bond running through the club."

SINCE then he has not looked back and has scored some memorable goals including a fantastic long range effort against Roma which proved to be the winner in their 1999/2000 UEFA Cup tie. "I think supporters like to see individual skills and I've always enjoyed attacking and running at the defence," says Harry. "It helps to get the crowd excited as well."

QUIZ QUESTION

WHEN HARRY WATCHED BRITISH SOCCER ON TELEVISION BACK HOME IN AUSTRALIA HE WAS A FAN OF WHICH CLUB? WAS IT LEEDS, LIVERPOOL OR MANCHESTER UNITED?

DURING the 2000/01 campaign he played a major part in Leeds' success in Europe, as well as in the Premiership. His big ambition at club level is to win the Premiership and the Champions' League in one season with Leeds. "I think we can push for what Man United have achieved," insists Kewell. "In the past four years we've finished in the top five in the Premiership every time, so we are getting closer and showing the consistency needed. This season, well you never know." Harry also wants to play in the World Cup finals with Australia. Considering he is still only 23 there is a good chance his dreams will come true.

KEWELL SIDELINES

WHEN HE SIGNED FOR LEEDS HE DID NOT TELL HIS PARENTS UNTIL AFTERWARDS.

HE IS CONTRACTED TO LEEDS UNTIL 2005 BUT HAS SAID HE WOULD LIKE TO ONE DAY PLAY IN SPAIN OR ITALY.

HE IS A FITNESS FANATIC AND HATES TO MISS DAILY TRAINING.

WHEN HE PLAYED FOR LEEDS' YOUTH AND RESERVE TEAMS HE WAS A LEFT-BACK BUT CHANGED POSITION WHEN HE WAS PROMOTED TO THE FIRST-TEAM.

KENNY MILLER
RANGERS

THEY SAID IT

Shoot is famous as the magazine that talks to all of the men who matter in the world of football, and the last 12 months haven't been any different. Here's what some of them have told us...

"There's very little chance of sustaining any kind of success with such a relatively small squad." The "never-satisfied" Martin O'Neill on why treble-winners Celtic must spend, spend, spend.

"All they needed was gloves and it would have been boxing." Claudio Ranieri on Chelsea's FA Cup battle at Highbury.

"I thought that if I took the potatoes off the hob United would equalise, so I ended up having to have mash. I ate mash again when we beat Sunderland, so I hope I had something to do with the wins." Trevor Sinclair discusses his, erm, magic spuds.

"If anyone thinks we've done enough already, they'd better think again." Man United defender Jaap Stam sends a worrying message to the rest of the Premiership.

"You have to perform two years on the trot before you can claim to be a top player." Ipswich's Marcus Stewart explains why 19 goals in your first campaign in the top flight is just not good enough.

"Stick with us. I can promise you we will be challenging for a place in Europe this season," Derby's Rory Delap stakes his claim.

"I'm proud we haven't bought foreigners," says Leicester's, erm, Turkish international Muzzy Izzet.

"I was in the job for 48 hours, and I think I was on the phone for 38 of those!" Bradford's Stuart McCall reveals the pressures of management.

"We are Leeds, and we should be capable of beating anyone - especially at home," £18 million defender Rio Ferdinand knows where he's at.

"I'm a perfectionist, and I'm still not happy with my game," Robbie Fowler (pic above) aims to keep getting better.

"We have to buck our ideas up - we can't keep getting away with it." Roy Keane (pictured below) on why Manchester United 'only' won the League by 10 clear points.

"When will I quit football? Maybe when I am in the pub team with my friends when I am 40!" Paolo di Canio (pic left) has no plans to call it a day.

"It'd be really special to win something with England - that motivates me every single day." David Beckham on what forces him to keep on improving.

EURO STARS

The Premiership might be the best league in the world, but it's not just in England that the stars shine. Right across Europe some of the world's best players can be found turning on the style.

Zinedine Zidane

Gabriel Batistuta

Oliver Kahn

ZINEDINE ZIDANE
Juventus & France

VOTED World Footballer of the Year twice in the last three years, Zidane is France's greatest player. His skills helped inspire France to win the 1998 World Cup and Euro 2000, as well as keeping Juventus at the peak of the Italian game. He began his career with Cannes and moved to Bordeaux before joining Juventus in the summer of 1996. Born in Marseille, Zidane says that his ambition is to play for his hometown club before he retires.

LUIS FIGO
Real Madrid & Portugal

IT is a measure of Luis Figo's standing in the game that it took a massive £37m to secure his transfer from Barcelona to bitter rivals Real Madrid in the summer of 2000. The driving force behind Portugal's thrilling performances over the last couple of seasons, Figo is a defender's nightmare. He is able to beat players on either side, shoot with both feet and conjure up chances out of nothing. Born in Lisbon, he began his career with Sporting and moved to Spain with Barcelona in July 1995.

RIVALDO
Barcelona & Brazil

THE 1999 World Footballer of the Year is one of the most skilful and exciting players you are ever likely to see. Handed Brazil's legendary number 10 shirt - always reserved for the most exciting performer in the side - he is an expert dribbler, brilliant passer and packs a powerful shot too. Having played for Brazil's top clubs he began his European career with Deportivo La Coruna of Spain. Often linked with Man United, he has admitted that: "One day I'd like to play in England, although at the moment I'm very happy at Barcelona."

GABRIEL BATISTUTA
Roma & Argentina

NICKNAMED 'Batigol' for his free-scoring ways, Batistuta is quite simply one of the most feared strikers of his generation. Quick and strong, he can shoot with both feet from any angle or distance and almost always hits the target. A legend at previous club Fiorentina - where fans erected a life-sized bronze statue of him outside the ground - he joined Roma for a whopping £22m in July 2000. Not a bad price for a 31-year-old!

PAOLO MALDINI
AC Milan & Italy

FROM the day he made his debut for Milan as a 16 year-old back in 1985 Maldini has been in the spotlight. By the age of 25 he had been involved in just about every major competition that world football can offer. The key to Maldini's class is that he is a model professional. A faultless defender at left-back or in the centre, he has skill, intelligence, pace and an on-pitch arrogance that only the truly great performers possess.

OLIVER KAHN
Bayern Munich & Germany

VOTED Man of the Match in last season's Champions' League Final after saving three Valencia efforts in the penalty shoot-out, Kahn has been a hugely impressive last line of defence for Bayern since 1994. He has also established himself as Germany's first choice over the last couple of seasons, after a head-to-head battle with Dortmund's Jens Lehmann. Solid and reliable, with great shot-stopping skills.

Paolo Maldini

Rivaldo

Luis Figo

THE LIGHT FANTASTIC

For the second season running, Sunderland found themselves one spot outside the European places last term. But they have made tremendous progress at the Stadium of Light in recent years and they are determined to go one step better this time around.

TROPHY HAUL

Sunderland fans will be hoping that 1998/99's Division One title win is the first of many to come. Here's a look at the Black Cats' complete trophy haul...

YEAR	TROPHY
1998/99	First Division
1995/96	First Division
1987/88	Third Division
1975/76	Second Division
1973	FA Cup
1937	FA Cup

IT is only two full seasons since Sunderland romped away with the First Division title to earn themselves a place back in the top flight after a two-year absence.

But it might as well be a lightyear, as the club have progressed beyond all recognition in that time to become one of the Premiership's leading sides and strong contenders for a European place for the first time since 1974.

From the scoring record of strikers Kevin Phillips and Niall Quinn through the midfield contributions of the likes of Don Hutchison and Gavin McCann and the goalkeeping of Thomas Sorensen, the Black Cats - even their nickname has changed with the times - have become a force to be reckoned with.

"We are an established Premiership side now, and it has been a long time since that was the case," admits manager Peter Reid, a former star with Everton and England.

"But now we have to take the next step and start winning trophies and qualifying for Europe."

One of the stars of last season's near miss was Don Hutchison, the tough but skilful Scotland international who was signed from Everton for £2.5m in July 2000. He echoes Reid's sentiments.

"I believe that we are good enough to make the Champions' League," insists Hutch. "And that is the aim of every one of the lads on the pitch, wearing the red and white stripes.

"Every game is a big game in this division and wherever we finish is where we deserve to, but no-one is working harder than us to get a Champions' League place."

Hutchison is in a good position to judge how well his current side are doing. In a career that began at Hartlepool in March 1990, he has played for Liverpool and Everton as well as enjoying spells with West Ham and Sheffield United.

And he believes that Sunderland can be every bit as powerful as reigning Champions Manchester United.

"Man United were unstoppable last season, but the chasing pack is getting stronger, with teams like ourselves, Liverpool, Arsenal and Leeds all improving by the year," he says.

"I reckon the next couple of years will see much closer title races.

"And there's no reason why Sunderland can't be part of that pack. Once we have gained a European place, big name players will be more likely to want to play at the Stadium of Light and we will continue to grow and get better."

One of the surprise successes of last season was the emergence of midfielder Gavin McCann as an England player - not bad for a lad who was bombed out of Everton for just £500,000 in 1998.

"It was an easy decision to join Sunderland, it's a really good set-up here," says McCann. "It's a club that's going places and it helps you as an individual when the team is doing well.

"As for playing for England, it was great, a fantastic experience. Who wouldn't enjoy playing for their country?

"But I'm not thinking about that right now. I'm concentrating on Sunderland - I want to play in every game and finish as high as we can."

Sunderland boss Peter Reid (above) points the way forward for England midfielder Gavin McCann (left)

DON HUTCHISON
SUNDERLAND

FOOTBALL CRAZY!

Welcome back to planet football. It's one of the oddest places in the galaxy to live! Here's a final look at some crazy stories from the football world.

Artwork: Barry Holmes, barry@meta-gb.com

DON'T EAT THE SEATS

Southampton were prevented from selling 9,000 red plastic seats from the Dell... because they were dangerous to eat!

European Commission rules stopped the sale because the seats' paint contained small amounts of a chemical called cadmium, which experts say can cause cancer if swallowed in large quantities.

Saints' marketing director Paul Blanchard said: "It's crazy. If it happened on April 1, everyone would think it was a joke".

Coming Next: don't drink the floodlights!

CHILD'S PLAY

Jason Dozzell was still at school when he came on as a sub for Ipswich in a game against Coventry in 1984.

Having left his school bag by the touchline, Jason went on and scored! At 16 years and 57 days he remains the youngest player to have netted a top flight goal in England.

LES'S PRESSIE

When Tottenham and England striker Les Ferdinand was just starting out he was sent on loan to Turkish side Besiktas to get some experience.

To celebrate his arrival the Turks sacrificed a goat on the pitch and daubed its blood on Ferdinand's forehead and boots to bring him luck!

SHOOT Monthly

STEVEN GERRARD
ENGLAND & LIVERPOOL

ENGLAND

THOMAS GRAVESEN
EVERTON

WORDSEARCH

Hidden in the giant wordsearch below are the names of 20 of the British game's top goalkeepers. You will find them diving vertically, horizontally, diagonally or even backwards. To give you a helping hand, we've found the first one for you...but can you catch the rest?

THE MEN IN GLOVES YOU ARE LOOKING FOR ARE:

Fabien BARTHEZ, Carlo CUDICINI, Tim FLOWERS, Paul GERRARD, Shay GIVEN, Shaka HISLOP, David JAMES, Paul JONES, Dean KIELY, Chris KIRKLAND, Nigel MARTYN, Mart POOM, Paul ROBINSON, Mark SCHWARZER, David SEAMAN, Thomas SORENSEN, Neil SULLIVAN, Nicky WEAVER, Sander WESTERVELD, Richard WRIGHT.

K	I	E	L	Y	A	N	E	S	N	E	R	O	S
W	E	S	T	L	E	T	A	G	G	B	H	T	L
E	S	M	A	R	T	Y	N	I	Q	O	O	M	P
S	N	L	O	B	V	W	R	V	A	A	A	A	A
T	O	U	H	K	T	D	Z	E	H	T	R	A	B
E	S	A	C	A	W	L	L	N	C	R	Y	H	O
R	N	N	N	U	A	R	H	T	D	F	I	S	A
V	I	A	A	O	D	P	I	F	R	S	C	U	R
E	B	S	Z	M	N	I	A	G	L	T	T	L	M
L	O	R	W	S	A	W	C	O	H	A	A	L	A
D	R	E	E	B	L	E	P	I	T	T	H	I	N
C	G	W	A	A	K	R	S	K	N	W	U	V	B
P	O	O	V	S	R	M	H	R	L	I	L	A	F
B	B	L	E	A	I	M	K	M	O	O	P	N	P
S	H	F	R	O	K	O	T	I	J	A	M	E	S
S	A	C	E	G	E	R	R	A	R	D	B	E	S
S	C	H	W	A	R	Z	E	R	S	E	N	O	J

Quiz Answers on pp110/111

KING KIERON

What could be better than starring as a first-team player for the local side all your mates go and watch? Not a whole lot, but once you have done that what could be better than making the news with club and country? That's the Kieron Dyer story in a nutshell, but of course there is much more to it than that.

KIERON was born in Ipswich on December 28th 1978 and since his family were big fans of the Blues it was not long before he was going with them to Portman Road. When he was two and a half he cheered Ipswich to their UEFA Cup triumph in 1981 under the guidance of Bobby Robson. Little did anyone know then, of course, that 20 years later Robson would be Kieron's boss.

Despite his Ipswich roots, Kieron was actually more of a Liverpool fan, as he explains: "They were the best team in the country back then. There were loads of great players in that Liverpool side and I loved pretending to be them when I was playing down at the park. But my favourite was John Barnes - he was real quality."

A great success at schools football with Westbourne High and the 4th Ipswich Boys Brigade, Ipswich soon signed Dyer on schoolboy terms and then as a youth

player when he left school. There were doubts about him making it, because he was so small, but as soon as manager George Burley saw him in action he was convinced that Kieron had what it takes to reach the top. "I owe Ipswich so much for taking me on and then making me a better player," explains Kieron. He made his England youth debut on April 29th 1996, in a 2-1 win over Portugal, and alongside him were stars like the three Michaels - Bridges, Ball and Owen.

Later that year, on Boxing Day, he had a Christmas bonus when he made his senior debut for Ipswich in a 3-1 win over Crystal Palace. He was still a youth player at that stage, but that soon changed when he signed full professional forms for Ipswich on January 3rd 1997. The champagne corks popped again when he scored his first senior goal, in August 1997 against Bradford. It was the first Ipswich goal of that season too.

KIERON could not do much wrong that season. On September 9th 1997 he made his England under-21 debut in a 1-0 win over Moldova and then on October 10th he scored the late winner in a 1-0 away win over Italy. The Dyer family and his friends had hardly stopped celebrating and they were still in party mood when Kieron stepped up another gear with a call to the England 'B' team. His first match for them ended in a 2-1 defeat by Chile, but in the very next game Russia were beaten 4-1. His only disappointment came in the First Division Play-Offs, with Ipswich missing out on promotion to the Premiership.

KIERON is pretty unique in that he has scored while playing with a broken leg. Starring for Ipswich against Watford on March 2nd 1999 he was injured but recovered to score in a 3-2 win. It was only when he was carried off still in pain that it was realised he had broken his leg!

HE soon recovered, though, and was called up to the full England squad before the end of that season. The 1999/2000 campaign started with a big bang in the life of Kieron Dyer. Leeds had been trying to sign him but Ipswich were not interested in the deal they offered. Then Ruud Gullit, manager of Newcastle, made a £6m bid that the club accepted and Kieron found himself heading for St.James' Park. His pre-season training suddenly changed to another club and he made his debut in a 1-0 defeat by Aston Villa on the opening day of the season. "It all happened so fast," he recalls. "One minute I was an Ipswich player, the next I was on my way up to Newcastle on a plane."

QUIZ QUESTION

KIERON'S FIRST GOAL FOR NEWCASTLE WAS IN A LOCAL DERBY ON AUGUST 25TH 1999. WAS IT AGAINST SUNDERLAND, MIDDLESBROUGH OR DARLINGTON?

IF that was not exciting enough, there was another call to the England senior squad and on September 4th 1999 he made his full debut in a 6-0 win over Luxembourg. When he went off with an ankle injury at half-time, the fans gave him a standing ovation. "It was a moment I'll never forget when I stepped out onto the Wembley pitch wearing an England shirt," says Kieron. "I still can't believe it."

DYER SIDELINES

HIS MIDDLE NAME IS COURTNEY.

HE SCORED ONE OF THE MOST SENSATIONAL GOALS EVER SEEN AT GOODISON PARK WHEN HE RAN THE LENGTH OF THE FIELD FROM HIS OWN GOAL AREA WITH THE BALL AND LOBBED THE EVERTON GOALIE. EVEN THE HOME FANS STOOD TO APPLAUD.

HE LIKES THE NEWCASTLE RESTAURANTS BUT STILL MISSES HIS MUM'S HOME COOKING.

RUUD Gullit left Newcastle two days after they had lost to arch rivals Sunderland, with Kieron scoring his first goal for the club in that 2-1 defeat, and Bobby Robson took over. In only his second game in charge the Magpies beat Sheffield Wednesday 8-0 and Dyer scored number five. "Bobby Robson is a legend," says Kieron. "It's as simple as that. I know he will have a big influence on my career because he has achieved so much in the game." Now Kieron Dyer is one of the most talked-about young players in the game.

Quiz answer: Sunderland

REPUBLIC OF IRELAND
2001

SHOOT
Monthly

WHO WANTS TO BE A FOOTY-AIRE?

OK, you've done the easy bit and now we're getting up to the seriously big prizes. You've done brilliantly to get this far - especially if you've still got any of your lifelines left. If you haven't used them - don't forget!

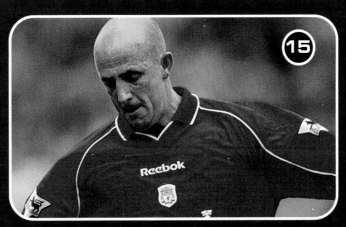

15

13 Win: The Champions' League
Q. David Seaman had the only what in the Premiership in 2000/01?

- A. Ponytail
- B. Moustache
- C. Green boots
- D. Hair extensions

14 Win: The European Championship
Q. Which two footballing personalities are family-related?

- A. Stuart Pearce and Ian Pearce
- B. Robbie Elliott and Matt Elliott
- C. Gary Kelly and Ian Harte
- D. Martin O'Neill and Keith O'Neill

15 To win: The World Cup
Q. At which club did Gary McAllister start his English career?

- A. Liverpool
- B. Coventry
- C. Leeds
- D. Leicester

13

Answers on page 110-111

QUESTION 13

PHONE THE COACH: a
SUB: Answers a and b are left.
ASK THE CROWD
A B C D

QUESTION 14

PHONE THE COACH: c
SUB: Answers c and d are left.
ASK THE CROWD
A B C D

QUESTION 15

PHONE THE COACH: d
SUB: Answers c and d are left.
ASK THE CROWD
A B C D

GIANFRANCO ZOLA
CHELSEA

104

THE LITTLE EMPEROR

Overseas players come and go - but Chelsea's Gianfranco Zola has put down his roots at Stamford Bridge.

Of the many foreign imports who have arrived on British shores since the Premiership kicked off in 1993, few have made a bigger impact than Chelsea's Gianfranco Zola.

Signed by Ruud Gullit for £4.5m from Italian club Parma in November 1996, the pocket-sized genius has impressed everyone in the game with his fantastic skills and his refreshing attitude - he always seems to have a smile on his face, both on and off the pitch.

Chelsea fans were devastated when rumours flew around west London last season that Zola was considering a return to Italy because his family were homesick. When the skilful Italian international announced he was going to remain at Stamford Bridge the supporters unfurled a banner thanking his wife, Franca, for letting him stay!

His popularity stems from much more than his undoubted brilliance on the ball. Zola has made every effort to fit in to the English way of life, even picking up the British sense of humour. When asked by reporters a few seasons ago how he enjoyed a game in which he had been particularly closely marked by Sheffield Wednesday defender Peter Atherton, Zola famously replied: "I prefer my wife."

While other big name imports have turned up, cashed their pay cheques and moaned about the way of life, Zola has quietly made himself at home.

"Since I've been in London I've found everything I wanted," he explains. "I am enjoying my time here".

But it is Zola's football which has really captured the imagination, and made him a hero at Stamford Bridge and beyond. Fantastic close control, wicked passing skills and a David Beckham-type accuracy from free-kicks - learned from endless hours on the practice pitch alongside Maradona when both were at Napoli - combine to keep fans on the edge of their seats.

It is no coincidence that the five years that Gianfranco has spent with Chelsea have been the most successful in the club's history, with the League Cup, European Cup-Winners' Cup and two FA Cups finding their way to Stamford Bridge in that time.

"There is a certain quality that is very important in England," says Zola, in an attempt to explain his popularity. "The will to make an effort and to make yourself an important team player.

"Above all I think you need to know how to put your qualities to the service of the team. I base my game on instinct, on invention.

"If you are not in a supportive environment, with a good team, then the lamp in your brain stops lighting."

Chelsea fans will be hoping that Zola's light keeps shining for a few more seasons yet.

THE LIFE AND TIMES OF GIANFRANCO ZOLA

1966 Born the son of a barman in the Sardinian village of Oliena.

1985 Joins Serie C2 side Nuorese, then signs for C1's Torres.

1989 Signed by Napoli for £200,000.

1990 Scores twice in 18 games as Napoli win Serie A.

1991 Makes his debut for Italy in a European Championship qualifier against Norway in February.

1993 £5m takes him to European Cup-Winners' Cup holders Parma.

1994 Helps Parma to a second successive ECWC Final, which they lose to Arsenal. Plays at the USA World Cup.

1995 Scores 19 goals in 32 League games, and five more in the UEFA Cup as Parma beat Juventus in the Final.

1996 Misses crucial penalty against Germany at Euro 96 as Italy go out in the group stage. Joins Chelsea for £4.2m.

1997 Scores Italy's only goal in their win against England at Wembley in a World Cup qualifier. Scores two sensational goals to help Chelsea win the FA Cup Semi-Final v Wimbledon and plays as Chelsea win the Final.

1998 Helps Chelsea to lift the Coca-Cola Cup. Comes off the bench to score the winner as Stuttgart are beaten 1-0 in the Cup-Winners' Cup Final.

1999 Top scores for Chelsea, with 13 League goals, as the Blues qualify for the Champions' League.

2000 Zola's back at Wembley as Chelsea win the FA Cup for the second time in three years.

LOTTERY WINNERS!

Tasting glory in the Play-Off Final is a bit like winning the national lottery - it can change a club's life and bring riches beyond their wildest dreams. Last season's winners are now enjoying a taste of the high life. Here's how they did it.

TROTTING TO THE PREMIERSHIP

THE term yo-yo club could have been invented for Bolton. Since 1992 the Trotters have been on a rollercoaster ride that even the craziest Disneyland inventor would consider too extreme. Their record reads something like this...up, up, up, down, up, down and now up again.

It certainly isn't boring being a Bolton fan, and thanks to goals from Gareth Farrelly, Ricardo Gardner and last season's top scorer Michael Ricketts in a 3-0 win over Preston at the Millennium Stadium, Wanderers have now trotted back into the top flight.

After two successive Play-Off defeats, the win came as a huge relief to manager Sam Allardyce, who admitted: "I can't put what I feel into words, it's like the world has come off my shoulders."

The First Division Play-Off Final is arguably the biggest single game in the domestic calendar, with the winners guaranteed a massive windfall of millions of pounds.

For last season's runners-up, Preston, the Play-Off Final was an unexpected bonus, and manager David Moyes said that he believed his young side would return stronger than ever.

"The difference was experience," explained Moyes. "I hope we'll learn from it and come back again."

Bolton will earn around £30m from rejoining the Premiership, but even that did not prevent the bookies from making them favourites to go straight back down again.

Mind you, they said that about Ipswich and Charlton, too.

SADDLED UP

READING were left cursing their luck as Walsall bounced straight back into the First Division via the Play-Offs.

The Saddlers had been relegated just 12 months earlier, but substitute Darren Byfield sealed their return with a 25-yard extra-time strike to give his side an unlikely victory.

It completed a remarkable turnaround for Ray Graydon's team, who had trailed the Royals 2-1 with 14 minutes of extra-time remaining.

But two strikes in a minute, from Byfield and a Tony Rougier own goal, turned the tie on its head.

Former Sunderland, Wolves and Bradford striker Don Goodman scored Walsall's first equaliser during the game - and then described the match as the most exciting of his career.

"I've played in an FA Cup Semi-Final and won the old Division Three in my first season as a pro with Bradford.

"But for sheer elation, entertainment and relief afterwards then winning this Play-Off is the high point of my career."

THE FUTURE IS TANGERINE

THERE is rarely such a thing as a dull Play-Off Final, and last season's Third Division battle was no exception.

Blackpool took thousands more fans to the Millennium Stadium, and in the end they took the glory too - but not before rivals Leyton Orient had given them an almighty scare.

The Os went ahead just 30 seconds into the game and were 2-1 in front as half-time approached, but ended up losing 4-2 as Blackpool powered forward after the break.

Ian Hughes, Brian Reid, Paul Simpson and Brett Ormerod were the heroes of the hour for Blackpool and manager Steve McMahon enjoyed the thrill of seeing his team win a showpiece final.

"If you could guarantee it, you'd choose going up via the Play-Offs every time," he said. "It makes your season."

THE BEST OF
LAST WORD
WHEN WAS THE LAST TIME YOU...

DANNY MURPHY
...WERE SPEECHLESS?

"That must have been when I turned to the referee in a Premiership game last year and said: "Ref, you're having a nightmare." He replied: "So are you son." There was no comeback to that, I was gobsmacked."

CURTIS FLEMING
...WERE SPOTTED IN THE STREET?

"It happens all the time. I was shopping once and a family asked if there was any chance of having their photo taken with me. I ended up going into the photo booth with them, one at a time!"

PAUL JONES
...SWAPPED SHIRTS WITH ANYONE?

"I do it all the time. I've collected some good ones in my time, like Peter Schmeichel and Claudio Taffarel of Brazil. I've got a few and they are all hung up on my wall."

MATT JANSEN
...GOT ANGRY?
"The last time that my brother-in-law beat me on my PlayStation! We are really competitive and we tend to have a few marathon sessions until one of us eventually wins."

ANDREI KANCHELSKIS
...PAID TO GO TO A MATCH?
"It was when England played Scotland at Wembley in the Euro 2000 Play-Offs. I had no problem getting a ticket for the game in Scotland, because I was playing for Rangers at the time and could get them through the club. But I paid for my ticket for the game at Wembley."

LEE HUGHES
...SCORED A HAT-TRICK?
"I've been lucky enough to score a few. I once scored two in seven days, which was special. I got three on the Saturday against Gillingham, then my wife had our baby, Mia, on the Monday and I scored another hat-trick on the following Saturday against Preston. I was floating on air that week, I can tell you!"

STEPHEN CARR
...MET SOMEONE FAMOUS OUT OF FOOTBALL?
"Met someone famous? I don't mix in those kind of circles! The last time I saw someone famous was last year when I was at Gatwick airport and I spotted the American actor Johnny Depp."

FROM PAGE 22

QUICK FIRE ROUND
1. Bolton. 2. Crewe. 3. Derby County.
4. Left-back. 5. Leicester. 6. Charlton.
7. Southampton. 8. Charlton (Mathias Svensson) v Everton (Paul Gerrard).
9. Fulham. 10. Steven Gerrard.

THE NAME GAME
1. Michael Owen. 2. Ruud van Nistelrooy.

FROM PAGE 76-77

LINK 'EM UP

Liverpool Anfield

Fulham Craven Cottage

Blackburn Ewood Park

Tottenham White Hart Lane

West Ham Upton Park

Ipswich Portman Road

GRID WORD
1. Play Offs; 2. The Valley; 3. Liverpool;
4. Division Three; 5. Crystal Palace; 6. Teddy Sheringham; 7. Henrik Larsson; 8. David O'Leary; 9. Bayern Munich; 10. Manchester United. Secret message: SHOOT IS ACE

WARP FACTOR
A. Mark Viduka; B. Emile Heskey;
C. Marcus Stewart; D. Gianfranco Zola;
E. Steven Gerrard; F. Kieron Dyer;
G. Michael Carrick; H. Henrik Larsson;
I. Claus Jensen.

WORD SEARCH

```
K I E L Y A N E S N E R O S
W E S T L E T A G G B H T L
E S M A R T Y N I Q O O M P
S N L O B V W R V A A A A A
T O U H K T D Z E H T R A B
E S A C A W L L N C R Y H O
R N N N U A R H T D F I S A
V I A A O O P I F R S C U R
E B S Z M N I A G L T T L M
L O R W S A W C O H A A L A
D R E E B L E P I T T H I N
C G W A A K R S K N W U V B
P O O V S R M H R L I L A F
B B L E A I M K M O O P N P
S H F R O K O T I J A M E S
S A C E G E R R A R D B E S
S C H W A R Z E R S E N O J
```

WHO WANTS TO BE A FOOTY-AIRE?

FROM PAGE 13
1.D. 2.C. 3.A. 4.B.
FROM PAGE 35
5.C. 6.B. 7.B. 8.A.
FROM PAGE 75
9.D. 10.A. 11.A. 12.B.
FROM PAGE 103
13.B. 14.C. 15.D.